HOW GREEN IS YOUR CITY?
Pioneering approaches to environmental action

Joan Davidson is a writer and consultant specialising in community-based environmental action in the UK and some Third World countries. She is a Research Fellow at the Bartlett School of Architecture and Planning, University College London. She also studied local environmental action as a Leverhulme Research Fellow (1981–83) and with a research fellowship from the Economic and Social Research Council (1985–86). She has been a consultant to UNESCO, OECD, the International Union for Conservation of Nature and Natural Resources and the Department of the Environment.

She has published many papers and books on conservation, including *The Livable City* (with Ann MacEwen, 1983) and *Women and Environment in the Third World* (with Irene Dankelman, 1988). She is a regular columnist for *The Guardian*.

Also published in the Community Action series:

Grassroots Initiatives: A Selection from New Society

HOW GREEN IS YOUR CITY?
Pioneering approaches to environmental action
Joan Davidson

Bedford Square Press

Published by
BEDFORD SQUARE PRESS of the
National Council for Voluntary Organisations
26 Bedford Square, London WC1B 3HU

First published 1988
© Joan Davidson, 1988

ISBN 0 7199 1215 6

Typeset by CRB Typesetting Services, Ely
Printed and bound in Great Britain by
Dotesios (Printers) Limited Bradford-on-Avon, Wiltshire

A CIP catalogue record for this book is available from
the British Library.

Contents

Preface

Environmental action offers no panacea for the city. It can only be one among many ingredients of regeneration. But the pioneering schemes described in this book show what is possible when people with energy and commitment first recognise and then work upon the assets of a neighbourhood.

Greening, energy saving, and waste recycling can all be valuable starting points, not only for transforming the image of run-down areas, but for bringing a new vitality to jobless and disheartened people. These pioneering schemes show how it is possible to be opportunistic with meagre environmental resources and slender budgets, while becoming increasingly responsive to the special needs of an area and its people – often bypassed by conventional inner city programmes. And the schemes are innovative in other ways – linking environmental and social action with the development of new jobs and enterprises. They see the city as people do: not as a set of compartmentalised activities, but in a holistic way, as a total environment for living.

Across Europe, environmental initiatives in the voluntary sector are pioneering ways of tackling urban decline, and European Year of the Environment has done much to publicise and celebrate their achievements. At the time of writing, inner city policy is again topical in the UK, and the community contribution to urban regeneration is steadily gaining more recognition. But the movement needs practical support and encouragement to achieve its potential and provide new hope for neglected areas and the communities that live in them. This book explores some of the ways in which this can happen.

Acknowledgements

Many busy people helped at various stages of this study with information, ideas and advice. I want to thank especially: Jon Aldenton and Terry Lyle (Tower Hamlets Environment Trust); Philip Barton (formerly Manchester Community Technical Aid Centre); Grant Blakemore (Blackwall Products); Sarah Buchanan (The Volunteer Centre); John Davidson (Groundwork Foundation); Robert Davies (Business in the Community); Jeff Cooper (London Waste Regulation Authority); Mike Croxford (Community Support Anti-Waste Scheme – CSAWS); Peter Downing (Dartington Institute); Nicholas Falk (URBED); Jo Gordon (National Council for Voluntary Organisations); Jenny Hendy and Hugh Barton (Urban Centre for Appropriate Technology); Robin Henshaw and Tim Edge (Oldham and Rochdale Groundwork Trust); Alan Hewitt (Neighbourhood Energy Action); Ute Jaeckel (Ashram Acres); Deirdre King (Keeping Newcastle Warm); Jan Kuiper (Paperback); Grant Luscombe (Landlife); Walter Menzies (Macclesfield Groundwork Trust); Mike Primarolo and Lin Whitfield (National Federation of City Farms); Chris Shirley-Smith (Growth Unlimited); William Solesbury (Department of Environment); Jane Stephenson and Richard Walker (Avon Friends of the Earth); Diane Warburton and David Wilcox (Partnership Ltd); Barbara Wheeler-Early (Free Form Arts Trust); Peter Wilmers (Rossendale Groundwork Trust).

I am grateful to the Economic and Social Research Council for funding under the Environmental Initiatives Programme and to Michael Collins and other colleagues at the Bartlett School of Architecture, University College London. This book also draws upon research supported by the European Foundation as part of a study of voluntary work in the environment.

Many others, too numerous to mention, gave time willingly to talk about their work and share their enthusiasms. Thanks to them for stimulating conversations, and apologies for any misinterpretations – my descriptions of the projects do not necessarily reflect the views of their organisers.

The Calouste Gulbenkian Foundation, the Groundwork Foundation and IBM UK Ltd have generously given financial support to the publication and launch of this book. Jackie Sallon, Gillian Whyte and Jonathan Croall at Bedford Square Press have provided many helpful ideas on the text and photographs.

Lastly, thanks to my family for all their support.

PHOTOGRAPH ACKNOWLEDGEMENTS

Out of the spent and unconsidered earth
The cities rise again.

(*from 'Cities and Thrones and Powers' by Rudyard Kipling*)

1 Introduction

THE URBAN CONTEXT

Urban areas in Britain have experienced fundamental changes over the last two decades. The flight of people and investment which has been accelerated by recession and cuts in public expenditure has left parts of many cities with jobless and disheartened communities, poorer services, neglected homes, much vacant land and a sharply declining quality in the local environment. Official figures in November 1987 registered 2.75 million as unemployed and claiming benefit in the UK. Although the number of jobless seems now to be falling, the real total is thought to be still some 3.3 million.

Aside from direct government and private sector action, many different community-based initiatives have emerged in response to these circumstances. They employ both volunteer and paid workers, and operate in what has generally come to be recognised as the 'voluntary sector'.[1] This makes up a relatively independent, self-managing 'third arm' of activity, neither governmental nor commercial – although there are frequently close links with both the public and the private sectors. Recent public policies have encouraged small-scale, partnership initiatives in the voluntary sector to start up in the inner city.

Many changes are also taking place in the way local social and environmental services are delivered which augment these trends. Reductions in public expenditure and a shift in the philosophies of caring have encouraged the development of services which devolve more responsibility to communities and self-help groups. The move from institutional to community care of those who are mentally ill is just one example. So, both by default and design, services are emerging which depend more and more upon action in the voluntary sector.

Third arm organisations are widening as well as deepening their involvement. Social services, concerned with health care, housing and the welfare of children, disabled and old people, still dominate the picture – a fact reflected in the growing membership of the voluntary sector's co-ordinating bodies, such as the National Council for Voluntary Organisations, and in the extensive literature on the voluntary sector.

But with the failure of conventional economic policies to do much to revive many local economies and provide jobs, there is increasing voluntary sector interest in local economic initiatives – both conventional small businesses and various kinds of community enterprise generated through the economic development programmes of local authorities and local enterprise agencies. There is substantial documentation on local economic initiatives which is beginning to show who starts them, how they develop and what their needs are.[2]

As the environmental movement strengthens, there has been a concern to apply its messages of resource conservation and sustainable development to the city, and this too has found practical expression at the local scale.[3] In terms of protest and campaigning for support, in fundraising and strengthening their membership, environmental groups have become increasingly successful over the last decade.[4] Their combined membership now totals more than three million. Of course, much of this is 'armchair participation' – an expression of sympathy for environmental causes and a willingness to contribute financially to them, which is not necessarily translated into practical action at the local level. But although only 4 per cent of the British population is thought to be actively engaged in environmental work, participation is growing rapidly.[5] More members of conservation groups want to 'do something practical' and many organisations established for other purposes (such as youth groups and pensioners' clubs) sometimes carry out environmental work – in response to local need, special awards or new funds.

PRACTICAL ACTION

A small but growing number of initiatives, arising locally, are concerned with environmental action as a major part of their work. They involve a variety of practical resource-conserving activities – energy-saving, waste recycling, the rehabilitation of buildings and the greening of vacant land. These initiatives most often deliver an environmental service locally; a few are concerned with the manufacture of products (usually from recycled materials). Some are trading these services and products and operating as environmental enterprises.

Any rigorous classification of community-based projects into social, economic, or environmental action is, in many ways, arbitrary – although government departments and funding sources do this. The pattern is complicated because social projects sometimes spin off environmental gains – associated for example with schemes for the community refurbishment of housing. And some projects which may originally have been stimulated by an environmental concern, such as local energy conservation schemes, have become dominated by social issues – in this case, fuel poverty. Community-based projects which can be said to be wholly or partly environmentally motivated seem to be very much in the minority, and to have received little attention – yet they offer some valuable lessons for other kinds of local action.

All these examples of social, economic and environmental activity arising in local communities provide the practical dimension to a growing body of (largely theoretical) research which argues that urban regeneration will only come about with greater local self-reliance and more emphasis upon economic development which is sustainable in social and ecological terms.[6] These ideas are seen as applying both to developed countries and the Third World, and there has been a consistent call for more documentation of practical examples from both hemispheres.[7] This book looks at local environmental action, in a number of different cities, as one ingredient of the movement towards greater self reliance. Job creation is another theme.

WORK AND THE ENVIRONMENT

There is much talk of environmental action as a potentially significant area of new work. One recent report estimates that some 200,000 jobs might be created overall, though mainly in pollution control.[8] This echoes previous studies that some 50,000 new jobs might flow from an intensive programme of energy conservation in buildings and an unspecified number of new jobs would accompany increased emphasis upon city greening. But there is little firm statistical evidence for the scale of present employment, or of new work that might be created, in the type of community-based action addressed in this book.

A study of environmental work for the Department of the Environment carried out by the Dartington Institute estimated that in 1984, some 250,000 volunteers contributed 1.6 million workdays and 36,500 people were employed on environmental action supported by the Manpower Services Commission.[9] Responding to the estimates of future work that could be created, the Department of Environment launched UK 2000 in 1986 which promised 5,000 full and part-time temporary jobs in environmental work, and more opportunities for volunteers.

It is not possible from the projects studied here to refine estimates of the total numbers working on environmental action at the community level. The cases confirm that the number of temporary workers can be substantial on any one scheme. The opportunities for permanent paid jobs are, so far, modest but capable of growth. This study concentrates instead on the kind of work local environmental action can generate, the benefits and some of the difficulties encountered. The interactions between volunteering and paid work are explored, for this interface is an important one in assessing future work patterns. One consequence of economic recession and present government policies is a blurring of the distinctions between paid and unpaid employment with a rapid expansion of 'marginal work' – in low paid and part-time jobs, in the informal economy and in temporary employment schemes and training projects organised by the Manpower Services Commission.[10] The future for environmental action at the local level is closely bound up with developments in volunteering and paid work.

FOCUS OF THIS BOOK

The research on which this book is based had three aims:

- to provide, through case studies, an environmental dimension to the experience that has been built up on social projects and local economic initiatives in the voluntary sector;

- to add further documentation on the environmental role of the community in cities;

- to augment ideas about the potential of environmental activity to provide work – both paid and unpaid, temporary and permanent.

Selecting good examples to report was not easy. The literature and early discussions showed that, for many people, environmental action has come to mean only 'greening'. 'Environment' seems to be interpreted almost exclusively in visual terms rather than, more holistically, as about improving the efficiency with which a number of local resources are used, and the multiple local benefits this might bring. The emphasis in this study was placed upon three types of environmental scheme: those concerned with city greening, with energy conservation and with waste recycling. These three classes of activity are all at a rather different stage of development but they have interesting experiences in common, and often face similar problems. Indeed some local schemes combine more than one type of environmental action, linking, for example, waste and energy management.

Housing rehabilitation and the conversion of industrial buildings to workspace and tourist facilities (although all these have environmental implications) were excluded from this study – they have been well documented elsewhere.

The projects discussed in this book were selected to represent some of the diversity of local environmental action; they include both large and small schemes, but concentrate on those that are essentially urban, operating in the inner city and in generally deprived neighbourhoods. All the projects selected tackle practical action – they deliver an environmental product or service in a particular locality rather than just campaign or fund raise for an environmental cause, although these are often subsidiary activities.

The perspective for analysis was the experience of *community groups* and their *projects* – those identified with a particular neighbourhood or set of neighbourhoods and involving people who live there as workers or users of the scheme. Many of the initiatives were helped, especially in the early stages, by *enabling groups*, also based locally (though concerned with more than one neighbourhood and many schemes), who provide advice and technical assistance, and are sometimes involved in executive work in creating or maintaining a scheme. The role of these technical aid groups was also investigated, but in connection with a local scheme rather than in a more general way. Similarly, where *national co-ordinating organisations* have been involved with a local scheme, their role is also discussed.

The following chapters deal in turn with the nature and diversity of environmental action at the local level, with the development of individual initiatives and how they have grown, with their role in work creation, and with some of the strengths and weaknesses they display. A final chapter sums up the ingredients of good practice and looks at the prospects for further development.

Because of their limited number, the projects included in this book, pioneering though they are, cannot truly represent the rich variety of environmental action in Britain's voluntary sector, especially among less formally organised groups. While some of the schemes involve ethnic minorities, it has proved especially difficult to locate environmental initiatives where they are the managers.

All the projects are changing – often rapidly – so the staff and financial figures given are necessarily indicative of development rather than the current position. And all are unique, adapting to fit the circumstances of the neighbourhood in which they operate. They are not suggested as general models of good practice that can be easily followed elsewhere, but rather as examples of how local people have responded – often with great energy and imagination – to particular problems and opportunities.

2 Local Environmental Action

In the social services, it has long been recognised that voluntary organisations can provide needed services effectively. That the voluntary sector can also deliver environmental services has been acknowledged more recently – and perhaps less readily. The notions persist that environmental organisations are primarily campaigners and fund raisers, are not in the business of service delivery, that they have little interest or expertise in running commercial enterprises, and that they can be poor staff and financial managers.

Undoubtedly, some organisations fit this mould, but recent years have seen major changes in the pattern of environmental activity at the local level, especially in cities. There is now much more practical action and it is increasingly diverse. Projects and their managing organisations defy easy categorisation for some involve many aspects of the creation, protection and management of environmental resources. There are initiatives concerned with improving and caring for open land, restoring the built environment (not just domestic and industrial buildings but urban structures such as canals and historic machinery), and with the conservation and recovery of natural resources. Excluding the built environment (for the reasons given on page 4), three categories are used here to review the range of activities that has developed and set the chosen case studies in context:

- activities associated with greening

- energy conservation

- waste recycling

CITY GREENING

The last two decades have seen an enthusiastic growth of urban greening which takes many forms, from the large-scale reclamation of industrial dereliction to the small-scale management of vacant urban plots.[11] In Liverpool, for example, Landlife – a local greening group – has transformed some 30 inner city sites from wasteland to wild habitats since the 'Greensight Project' began in 1979.[12] Here, as in other British cities, the work is varied – with tree, shrub and flower planting, the care of woodlands, the clearing of ponds and litter.

The urban greening movement involves both protection and creation. It includes conserving many of the remaining wild spaces that may be threatened. But there is also work to create new habitats for educational and community use. In both fields – conserving and creating – the British Trust for Conservation Volunteers is now a major agency for organising practical environmental action, often working in partnership with others – Groundwork Trusts for example. The 13 Trusts are part of an expanding network of local partnerships between the voluntary sector, business and local authorities, all working together to redeem derelict industrial and farming landscapes within and on the edge of urban areas.[13]

Not all creative work is directed towards natural habitat creation, although many schemes incorporate an ecological element, especially those associated with schools. Community gardens, including informal greenspace, play areas and often vegetable-growing, are a popular objective for local groups working on small sites (see the examples of Tower Hamlets Environment Trust, page 96 and Hackney Grove Garden, page 60). And not all the changes are permanent: some urban wasteland may be in the process of being built upon, but this has not prevented groups (like Landlife) from converting it temporarily for local use.

Urban greening increasingly involves the use of wasteland to produce food – in city farms and community gardens – such as are described in the case studies for Ashram Acres, page 10 and Windmill Hill, page 33. Windmill Hill, one of the earliest city farms, has just celebrated a decade which has seen the movement grow from two farms in 1976 to nearly 60 in 1987. The National Federation of City Farms – a national co-ordinating body – has a widening membership of farms and community gardens and is busy helping them not only to extend their role as social and education centres, but to develop small businesses based on food production, horticulture and crafts. Many other voluntary groups have been encouraged to introduce green features in their neighbourhoods through special grant programmes such as the Shell Better Britain Campaign.

The worsening social and environmental condition of many inner- and outer-city housing estates has stimulated some communities to renovate their neighbourhoods in ways which combine work on land and buildings. Landwise, for example, is pioneering a new approach to the dismal back courts of Glasgow's peripheral housing estates. Working with tenants, Landwise aims not only to transform the wastelands around their homes with community gardens, allotments and playspaces, but create local jobs in doing so. Murals, greenspace and other improvements of the kind that have taken place at Sholver in Oldham (page 51) and on the Provost Estate in Hackney (page 93) are beginning to transform these run-down housing areas. And 1¼ million families live on estates classified in this way. Valuable ingredients of this work are celebrations and festivals which can do much to restore local pride in these neglected, often dangerous environments. Celebrating the urban green is a major activity of the national 'Think Green' campaign, based in Birmingham, which works with local groups to promote special events.

ENERGY CONSERVATION

During the 1970s, environmental groups became increasingly concerned about the state of the global environment and the escalating consumption of natural resources. In the aftermath of two oil crises, a number of practical energy conservation experiments began in several conurbations. Friends of the Earth groups, first in Newcastle and then in a number of other cities, pioneered local projects in which volunteers insulated the homes of old and disabled people (see Keeping Newcastle Warm, page 15).

In May 1981, the National Council for Voluntary Organisations (NCVO) initiated, with government backing from the Department of Energy and the Manpower Services Commission, a Neighbourhood Energy Action scheme, extending these ideas to other areas. The early initiatives have now become part of a national programme of more than 400 local energy projects offering insulation and energy advice to those on low incomes, co-ordinated nationally by Neighbourhood Energy Action (NEA – an independent charitable company since 1985) and Energy Action Scotland. All the local energy projects now involve paid labour (most use MSC special employment programmes) but they continue to be sponsored by voluntary agencies and some are still helped by volunteers.[14] Some 8,000 people are employed and more than 300,000 homes have been insulated.

Community involvement at a very local scale has been a key ingredient, vigorously promoted by NEA in its co-ordinating role. Close contact between insulating teams and their clients has become the principal source of finding other homes to tackle. And the teams have diversified their activity into giving energy and other advice locally, training, and assisting in job and business creation. Sometimes, as with the Urban Centre for Appropriate Technology in Bristol, an initial preoccupation with energy saving has become the stimulus for a whole range of conservation activities involving land and buildings (page 38).

NEA, like other national co-ordinating bodies, plays an important part in the development of local projects in the network – negotiating for favourable policy changes at national level and providing information and training to sustain high quality work.

WASTE RECYCLING

Rising unemployment has given an extra impetus to resource conservation schemes, like waste recycling, that generate jobs and offer opportunities for training in new skills. Most community-based recycling initiatives began and are still organised in the voluntary sector although many involve close working relations with local authorities.[15]

Initiatives are diverse, ranging from house collections of separated domestic waste (especially paper and rags), helping local authorities with the running of bottle and can banks, to workshops – often tucked away in city back streets – which refurbish furniture and other domestic goods, or collect scrap materials from industry for children's play (see the examples of Avon FOE, page 18, Community Support Anti-Waste Scheme (CSAWS), page 55, and Hackney Brass Tacks, page 70).

Although many recycling schemes now employ paid workers (most on MSC schemes), they rely, as CSAWS does in Cardiff and Brass Tacks in Hackney, on voluntary consumer sorting of wastes for home collections or on voluntary deposits of waste materials at recycling centres. Some schemes use volunteers to collect and sort wastes. A few small independent businesses are beginning to emerge (see Blackwall Products, page 78, and Paperback, page 80). The number of local recycling schemes has fluctuated over the last decade with the rise and fall of raw material prices: those relying on collections of low grade waste paper have been particularly vulnerable.[16] But overall, schemes have increased.

In some ways, although their number is greater, recycling schemes are at a similar level of development now as local energy schemes were in 1981. Until recently, there was little recognition of their role outside the local areas, no national promotion, co-ordination or financial support, and no formal training programmes building on the considerable experience which has been accumulated locally. Now, a new national initiative – Waste Watch, based at NCVO – is working to provide these supports, promote more community-based recycling schemes and lobby nationally for an extension of waste saving.

Ashram Acres

1 Doreen Brown and her grandson feed the geese at Ashram Acres, Sparkbrook.

Ashram Acres is a land use project in Sparkbrook, Birmingham – Britain's second city. Its aim is to blend local resources – of vacant land and people's skills and time – in growing food for a multi-racial community. The scheme is run entirely by volunteers and has become the focus for many new initiatives in the neighbourhood.

Sparkbrook is an inner-city area close to the centre of Birmingham, with many immigrant families from Pakistan, the West Indies and Eire. Hit hard by the recession and especially by the decline of manufacturing industry, much of its workforce is unemployed: up to 67 per cent of economically active men in some areas. Bad housing and poor services compound the poverty. Educational and medical provision are far below the national average, families are large, infant mortality rates high and there is much petty crime. At the start of this decade, the prospects for regeneration were slender and the community felt hopeless.

In 1982, Ute Jaeckel and Gill Cressey, both with experience of community work and race relations, moved into a vacant property in Grantham Road – a street of near-derelict Victorian houses with unusually large back gardens. They became the nucleus of a community dedicated to a resourceful style of living and to finding some way through the problems of the neighbourhood. Others joined in to form the Ashram Community Service Project (ACSP) which became a focus for community activity and they began to work out with local people what was needed most.

'We looked,' says Gill Cressey, 'not just at the problems but to the assets of the neighbourhood – its land and people'. Although most of the unemployed workforce were registered as unskilled at local job centres, they were in fact equipped with countless skills learnt from their childhood in rural farming families. They knew how to tend crops and had a variety of craft skills. Members of the project studied these, both in the neighbourhood and on a visit to related families in Pakistan and later began to develop a number of practical job-creating initiatives based on traditional skills. Improving training and the conditions of homeworking were important goals.

The terraced houses in Grantham Road continued as a base for the Ashram Community Service Project. Behind the houses, the partly tarmacced back gardens were known to local children as 'the jungle': land was vacant and neglected. In November 1981, as a pioneering scheme to show what might be possible, two gardens were dug up by the Ashram community, with help from local people, and planted with vegetables, including Asian and West Indian varieties. The first harvest was a success and the project's momentum grew. An adjacent garden was brought into cultivation in 1982, and two more gardens of houses due to be demolished were given by the City Council in 1983. Goats were bought (with the expenses shared) and goat's milk and cheese were produced for sale.

How it works

Since those early days, the project has spread in area and widened its activities. Sparkbrook has many large unused gardens and dere- lict sites awaiting development. Ten gardens now make up Ashram Acres, most growing a rich variety of fruit and vegetables, the rest grazed by goats. Asian vegetables – okra, mooli, karella and others – are a speciality and all are organically grown. The project now keeps geese, rabbits, chickens and bees; local children call it 'the farm'.

Ashram Acres grows a larger variety of crops than would be economic for its size, in order to demonstrate the possibilities. There are experiments with pest control, composting and different crop growing methods – using raised beds, greenhouses and polythene tunnels to improve production. Local people who visit are encour- aged to watch new developments and copy them. And the project tries to show how equipment can be cheaply made: a greenhouse was built from old window frames, polythene domes have been made by hand, plants are grown in old tyres. Ashram Acres will propagate seeds for use in other gardens and its members help to clear new gardens for cultivation. The project promotes a conserving style in other ways: solar panels heat part of the greenhouse and a workshop. Methods of cooking and preserving food are also demonstrated.

Ashram Acres is particularly sensitive to women's needs: even those who keep strict purdah can tend a goat in their own backyards and thereby participate in the project.

Funding and management

The two houses used as the original base for the Ashram Community Service Project were given on a short-term renewable lease from Birmingham City Council. A small staff was funded under the Inner City Partnership (a joint central and local government programme) and from Birmingham's Economic Development Unit. ACSP now has four full-time paid workers, and two job-sharing part-time.

But Ashram Acres – the vegetable project – has no paid staff. It is worked and organised entirely by volunteers. Grants have been neither sought nor received for fear that financial dependence would impose unwanted controls and destroy the scheme's capacity to experiment with new ideas. There is a core membership of 15 who presently pay £2.70 each week and work voluntarily in the gardens in return for as many vegetables as they need. Families with more dependants take more food and work longer hours. Others in the neighbourhood, who are not members, also come to work in the gardens and buy the produce. Prices are fixed in relation to those in local shops.

The aim is not to expand the core membership beyond 20, but for Ashram Acres to act as a working model to inspire local imitation among those who have rights of use and access to other sites. Only two members work regularly in the gardens every day, others come when they wish and join the busy Saturday 'work ins'.

Vegetable growing, the greenhouse and the animals are managed as separate financial units by three teams of members who report to a fortnightly members' meeting. Administration is shared and there are few 'rules': all is based upon mutual trust – that the project's users will not abuse the system. But there are dangers and some experience of volunteer 'burn-out'; the work is hard and continuous, for many families are now dependent on the food. 'The gardens,' says Ute Jaeckel, 'set their own demanding agenda. Our dreams of new developments are tempered by the daily pressures of reality, and the lack of paid staff can mean severe gaps are left when a skilled volunteer has to leave.' Ashram Acres would welcome trained secondees, more skilled long-term volunteers with their expenses paid, and international exchanges with similar projects.

There is a good deal of local support. The City Council has provided some help since the project began, first with buildings, later with land. No local byelaws exist to restrict cultivation or the keeping of animals: the project has always met the standards required by the city's Environmental Health Department. Ashram Acres Community Service Project has provided small amounts of capital to buy equipment; some, like the greenhouse, has been donated.

Benefits

Ashram Acres is much more than a land reclamation project. It makes use of wasted land and wasted skills in a way that has meaning for local people: food is a major item of their budget, fresh vegetables are a vital source of vitamins and minerals in generally impoverished diets. There are many related benefits – improvements to health, opportunities for rewarding work, for learning, play and sociable activity, for more self-reliance and self-esteem. For Mukhta Khan, with ill health and six young children, gardening is therapeutic as well as economic: 'It feels good to be here, there is a job for everyone.' His children come with others to play and help in the evenings, and join in the social activities which are an important feature of Ashram Acres: many religious festivals, birthdays and other events are celebrated. Doreen Brown, a founder member of the project, thinks the older people especially value these reminders of life in their native countries; for her, the gardens recall St Kitts where she was born.

Ashram Acres is a unique meeting place where people who differ widely in age, race, class, culture and background can work together. Hundreds of people – all volunteers, some physically and mentally handicapped – have been involved with the project so far, cultivating, maintaining, buying, selling, giving advice and gaining experience. People call in from around the world: there is a feeling of international significance to this local example of self-reliance.

The project remains the pioneering focus for ideas to be tried out before they are adopted in other gardens, and on more patches of vacant land in the neighbourhood. There are plans to experiment with butterfly breeding, silk production, herb growing and the use of vegetable dyes. Ute Jaeckel believes it is important to sustain enthusiasm by innovation and continual learning.

The project's major strength has been – and remains – its core of committed volunteers. Those who gave the initial leadership are still involved and live on the site in the ACSP house (incidentally providing security for the gardens).

In part, the success of Ashram Acres has persuaded Birmingham City Council to support a new job creation project in the neighbouring district of Smallheath – Ashram Asian Vegetables. Two and a half acres of derelict land are being used to grow Asian and West Indian vegetables organically, employing 102 of the area's long-term unemployed. The City Council, through its Economic Development Unit, is investing £126,000 in the scheme; with wages in the first year paid by the Manpower Services Commission under its Community Programme.

The year 1987/88 is a pilot period in which methods and markets for the produce are being explored, and participants are being trained. The hope is that new small businesses and permanent jobs, in horticulture, management and catering, can be established in subsequent years, when start-up finance will be available from the City Council for potentially viable schemes. Already, two new small businesses seem likely to develop using the Enterprise Allowance scheme. In its first year, the project is working closely with local 'caring' institutions such as hospitals, schools and children's centres, offering them free vegetables as well as training in how to cook them properly.

Keeping Newcastle Warm

2 *Over 400 local energy projects, like Keeping Newcastle Warm, provide jobs, training and practical help for low-income families.*

One of the first local energy projects, Keeping Newcastle Warm, has insulated some 22,000 homes on Tyneside. It has grown from a staff of 16 in 1980 to 107 in 1987.

In 1980, Newcastle City Council (a leading local authority on energy conservation) already had an extensive insulation programme for public housing. But the evidence from social surveys and voluntary organisations showed that low income households in privately owned and rented properties could also be helped by loft insulation and draught-proofing. Keeping Newcastle Warm (KNW) was established in 1980 to insulate these homes.

KNW works mainly in the inner city and with pensioners, disabled families and DHSS claimants. It offers heating advice, a free energy survey to assess the action needed, assistance with applications for grant, and then loft insulation (for owner occupiers), draught-proofing (which is also offered to council tenants as this is not covered by the council's insulation programme) and simple double-glazing.

Most clients do not pay for draught-proofing. They have been eligible for DHSS single payments or assisted by one of Newcastle's

14 Priority Area Teams. But from April 1988, all DHSS single payments are abolished. The draught-proofing allowance is replaced by an energy grant from the Manpower Services Commission, although this covers only 90 per cent of the costs of materials (not 100 per cent as under the old single payment system).

Heating advice is an important part of the work and is available on all the heating systems used in the city. Heating advice is linked where necessary to help with welfare rights, fuel debt and home security. KNW's insulation teams also do minor house repairs or refer clients to the relevant local authority department.

The project aims for high quality insulation: an independent consultant calls back on 1 in 10 homes after a month to check the work and clients are encouraged to complain if necessary.

Insulation materials are bought from ConservAction – a separate community-based trading co-operative (originally set up by KNW) which buys materials in bulk (and with discounts) to sell on to a number of local energy projects in the north east. ConservAction employs six and has an annual turnover of more than £300,000.

Most clients contact KNW after learning about its services from friends; half of all referrals are by word-of-mouth. Others come via voluntary sector and statutory agencies, local authority departments and the Priority Area Teams. KNW staff try to reach people who need the service through talks to pensioners' clubs and other groups, and the project is well publicised in the local media, and by posters in surgeries, libraries and community centres. Some people are referred by Crime Prevention Officers and Victim Support Groups.

Funding and management

Funding for Keeping Newcastle Warm comes from the City Council (through Inner City Partnership) and from the Manpower Services Commission. In October 1987, KNW became an MSC Managing Agency with a staff of 107 (four funded through the Inner City Partnership, and the rest through the Community Programme). Project security and diversity have increased and the agency now has five project teams providing:

- draught-proofing and insulation

- heating advice

- home security – a popular service with Newcastle's elderly, single people

- care and repairs for owner occupiers

- central administration

The Partnership funding for four permanent staff (project manager, deputy, administrator and finance officer) allows continuity of management to be maintained. The MSC participants are managed in small teams and encouraged to suggest improvements to all operations. Morale is high and about 50 per cent go on to permanent full-time jobs after the MSC year. There has been full discussion with unions over pay and conditions, and successful negotiations have allowed KNW to draught-proof council properties.

KNW is a non-profit company, limited by guarantee and is managed by an independent committee of representatives from the City Council (including Housing and Priority Area Teams, Social Services) and voluntary organisations (such as Neighbourhood Energy Action and Age Concern).

The project keeps in close touch with many other agencies locally. Fuel Boards, consumer councils and the DHSS assist with the training of new KNW advisory staff, and links with the City Council are strong – there are energy advice surgeries in some local housing offices and KNW has a desk in the city's Energy Information Centre – a 'one-stop shop' for energy advice. KNW rents premises from the City Council who also provide storage space and help the project to produce publicity materials. KNW staff are represented on the executive committee of the local Council of Voluntary Service, and on the boards of management of two other caring agencies so there is much pooling of information and experience.

To help local groups with the high cost of heating their buildings, KNW and ConservAction together established the Community Buildings Insulation Project. Operating in Newcastle and Gateshead, this scheme offers a free survey and insulation service to voluntary organisations.

Avon Friends of the Earth

3 Using play materials collected by the Children's Scrapstore at Avon FOE.

In Bristol, Avon FOE Ltd run a compendium of resourceful projects concerned with waste recycling and energy conservation – aiming to increase these activities locally and raise awareness. Some are MSC funded, others operate as self-financing enterprises.

In 1983, Bristol FOE joined with five other local FOE groups to form Avon FOE Ltd, a charitable company with a board of management chaired by Richard Walker: 'We wanted a more professional organisation, which could practise as well as campaign about conservation!'

Since 1980, Bristol FOE had collected waste paper (first voluntarily, then under a YOP scheme) taking over the city council's collections when they were withdrawn. In 1983, the newly-formed Avon FOE sponsored an MSC CP scheme to make house-to-house collections of domestic wastes – paper, rags, and sump oil – which were sold to merchants. This was the beginning of Resourcesaver, now an 80-place MSC scheme – one of a number of resourceful MSC projects for which Avon FOE is Managing Agent. These are:

- Resourcesaver

- Recycling workshops – renovating donated office furniture and making goods from reclaimed timber

- Scrapstore – collecting commercial and industrial wastes for use as children's play materials

- Management team – responsible for recruitment, training, health and safety and management advice

- Sustrans – a project promoting cycling as a sustainable mode of transport, mainly concerned with building cycle paths

And also under the Avon FOE umbrella are:

- Recycling Collective – a three-person partnership making household collections of waste paper, sump oil, rags and aluminium

- Arboreta Papers – a three-person business dealing in recycled paper products

- Energy Services – a five-person energy advice and installation firm

All these share the common goal of promoting resource conservation, and many of the projects' personnel also work voluntarily on FOE campaigning and management. The independent enterprises covenant part of their profits to support the work of Avon FOE. There is a strong element of mutual aid: most projects share the same building and office services; they use and promote each others' products, for example recycled papers and renovated furniture. In future, chairman Richard Walker and others envisage Avon FOE continuing to act as a catalyst for further self-sustaining enterprises. The main conservation projects are discussed in turn below.

Resourcesaver
Four lorries and two horse-and-cart teams operate five days a week to make monthly collections from homes and offices in Bristol, Bath and Chew Valley. The sale of all grades of paper (some 120 tonnes a month), rags and sump oil makes £2,000 each month in an area with some of the highest waste disposal costs in the UK. Avon County Council – the waste collection authority – pays Resourcesaver £1.76 for each tonne of paper collected – a token contribution for reducing the waste stream.

Horse and cart collections are cost effective and especially valuable for publicity. Low-cost stabling is provided by the City Council and the £60 per week food bill is a considerable saving on what would be required to run, tax and insure extra vehicles.

Public response to the collections is good and growing – in some areas attracting 7 out of 10 households to participate. Promotion is by leaflet drops, neighbourhood meetings, awareness-raising events and local media publicity. And part of the Resourcesaver team works with schools, encouraging them to collect waste and to use recycling as a teaching theme.

One aim is to increase the collection of higher value office papers from commercial firms. Resourcesaver already collects from Avon County Council, the Magistrates Court and a number of small businesses, supplying specially labelled fire-proof drums (salvaged from a chemical works). Aluminium is now also collected on the rounds, and research continues on the feasibility of collecting precious metals and plastics. Resourcesaver has recently collaborated with the council to establish bottle banks in the city, having earlier prepared a feasibility study on local glass recycling.

Under the MSC Community Programme, 80 people are employed – most part-time. Work on the house-to-house collections can be monotonous, but there are efforts to increase satisfaction by encouraging the collection teams to share their tasks, monitor progress, promote recycling and survey attitudes. In a recent development, the collections in rural areas and in central Bristol have become two smaller, self-managed units, to encourage participants to assume more responsibility for project performance and to evaluate the potential for these schemes to become self-sustaining enterprises (like the present Recyling Collective – see below).

Recycling workshops

This project employs 25 people on the Community Programme (including four full-time). Participants learn basic carpentry skills, make simple goods (shelves, rabbit hutches, bird tables) for sale from waste timber, or renovate office furniture for voluntary organisations. And they make other items for community use – including aids for the handicapped. Recent work has included the renovation of carts used on the waste collection rounds. But this is a training rather than a production centre: a number go on to learn further skills. Variety is introduced by varying the length of jobs, and through the interchange of personnel between the workshops. Two employees are seconded to another local organisation which restores discarded household furniture for low income families.

As with other renovation schemes, finding adequate supplies of good furniture to restore is a problem: veneered desks and modern filing cabinets do not recycle well. And as this is a CP scheme, there are no incentives to run the workshops as a business. With careful selection of staff and goods to be renovated, and more attention to demand and marketing, it is possible that the workshops could be self-financing – perhaps by concentrating on a repair service and making new furniture from waste. Changes proposed for the Community Programme could encourage this development.

Scrapstore

The Children's Scrapstore collects discarded industrial and commercial wastes to be transformed into materials for play. Paper, packaging, wood, paint, everything from buttons to BBC scenery has been scrounged for sale (at low prices) to nearly 700 local groups involved in caring for young children. Some play materials are bought in bulk for distribution at low cost, and equipment such as a badge-maker is available for hire.

Started by FOE, the Scrapstore now employs 12 Community Programme staff (4 full-time) and is part-funded by Urban Aid (which supports 3). Charitable status, with a separate trading company, allows the group to bid for other funds and generate extra income from training workshops for playleaders and the sale of goods from scrap.

Management

Overall, in this compendium of projects, some 200 people are employed under the Community Programme, most part-time, with 58 full-time staff including supervisors. Most are paid less than £2.50 per hour to accommodate the stipulated CP average of £67 per week. Women are well represented among the management staff, those working with schools and on the maintenance team. And the Recycling Workshops provide training opportunities for those who often find it harder than most to find employment, including some, for example, who are disabled.

Staff training is mainly organised, outside working hours, through the Avon Training Agency but all receive a half-day induction programme which includes a discussion of environmental issues. Participants discuss their progress and training needs regularly, and all are counselled about job searching. Now that Avon FOE has the extra resources that come with being an MSC Managing Agency, it is hoped the amount of environmental training can be increased, to improve staff involvement and commitment to the ideals of the recycling projects.

Large projects (like Resourcesaver) are managed in small teams. Project leaders meet monthly and report to the MSC Agency Management Team, which is responsible for overall direction. The board of Avon FOE Ltd, on which are represented the MSC Agency, the other independent enterprises (such as Energy Services) and Avon FOE's Campaigns Director, also meets monthly, to consider the direction and finances of the whole compendium of initiatives. In addition, the recycling activities are guided by an informal advisory committee of FOE recycling, development and campaigns staff and the paper merchant with whom Resourcesaver deals.

Recycling Collective

In the spring of 1985, a team of four who had worked as MSC participants on Resourcesaver (and faced uncertainty about future employment) became self-employed on the MSC Enterprise Allowance scheme. They formed a partnership and began making collections of paper, rags and oil in areas of Bristol where the public response was especially good. Three years later, the team (now three) is still trading and is self-financing – although paper prices have fallen. The team has recently introduced paper banks in small outlying towns from which they collect monthly.

Andy Cunningham, one of the partners, admits 'The work is intrinsically boring, but our commitment is high and we keep up morale by trying to improve performance and by talking with people on the rounds about recycling.' There is a variety of expertise in the team, including management, accountancy and computing. They have an answering machine and one lorry and collect 80 tonnes of waste per month.

Arboreta Papers

This independent enterprise deals in a variety of recycled papers, selling directly to local schools and firms and through shops in Bristol. With a £150,000 turnover, the business is small but expanding: last year saw a tenfold increase in the sale of recycled paper for duplicating. A subsidiary company, Rollcall, has been created to deal in recycled sanitary papers; and it is planned to market biodegradeable detergents.

Arboreta is one member of a consortium of recycled paper merchants which includes other FOE enterprises and Paperback (see page 80). Members benefit by ordering supplies in bulk from manufacturers, so reducing the price. They share ideas about marketing and avoid competition by dealing with different outlets.

Energy Services

This collectively managed enterprise offers an energy advice and installation service (for loft and cavity wall insulation and heating controls) mainly to domestic householders in Avon. With an annual turnover of some £80,000, it sustains five people working full-time, and provides part-time work for two self-employed insulation installers (who draw on a pool of self-employed builders). Two of the five who work full-time are based at the FOE offices and comprise an installations manager and energy adviser. Three other agents make free home heat loss surveys in advance of any further advice or installation work.

Operations are closely linked to those of the Urban Centre for Appropriate Technology (UCAT) and the Bristol Energy Centre (page 38) for mutual promotion and to avoid duplication. All the energy services are jointly promoted in a leaflet and there is much cross referral: the Energy Services team, for example, refer clients for draught-proofing to BEAT and to the technical advice available in UCAT. UCAT's 'low energy house' refers visitors to Energy Services, whose staff are used in the energy workshop.

Although there is no shortage of properties to be insulated in Bristol, marketing Energy Services is acknowledged to be difficult.

The team relies on referrals from the local authority, citizens advice bureaux, UCAT and others, and on responses to the free heat loss surveys. Energy Services leaflets are distributed by Resourcesaver and the Recycling Collective, and through local surgeries and the media. More effort is planned on promotion (for example, through talks) to reach the middle- and higher-income groups for whom the service is mainly designed.

In many ways this operates as a community business, for social objectives as well as profitability are important. Low- as well as higher-income clients are advised about energy matters and referred if necessary to sources of help with house repairs. Objectives have to be carefully traded off to maintain profitability – at times the team receive requests for surveys from low-income clients who must be referred elsewhere for the job to be done. And work in homes is highly seasonal: Energy Services relies on insulating commercial premises and private schools during the slacker summer months.

3 Starting Up, Keeping Going

In all the cases studied for this book, action has been triggered in a variety of ways. The following four are the most common.

● *Reacting to a threat.* In the greening schemes, local people have often come together to oppose a development and subsequently they organise action to improve the site – clearing litter, planting trees, creating a city farm or community garden (as at Windmill Hill, page 33, Sholver, page 51, and Hackney Grove Garden, page 60).

● *Reacting to opportunities.* Sometimes tenants, residents and other local groups act spontaneously to improve their neighbourhood or school as on the Provost Estate (page 93). The objective is first to tackle problems, later – and usually with outside help – to respond to opportunities. The role of local technical aid groups (in this case the Free Form Arts Trust) has been vital in these schemes, for they have articulated community priorities, suggested design solutions, and organised the funding, construction and management. Continuing community involvement is hoped and planned for, though not always easy to achieve.

● *Applying expertise.* Professionals (environmentalists and others – such as artists and community workers – exploring an environmental dimension of their skill) may unite to take action. Their motivation is both to respond to wasted opportunities perceived locally and also to seek practical ways of demonstrating their environmental preoccupations, which might also be used in campaigning. Landlife, for example, with the Greensight projects, wanted to show how low cost 'ecological' greening could work on wasteland sites. The 'low energy house' of Bristol's Urban Centre for Appropriate Technology (page 39) has become a practical demonstration of how a terraced property can be adapted for resource saving. Both of these were new organisations; sometimes a demonstration of this kind is organised through an existing local branch of a national campaigning body – recycling and insulation activities began this way in Avon, Newcastle and other Friends of the Earth groups (pages 18–23). Hackney Brass Tacks began as one of a number of workshops set up by the Mutual Aid Centre to show how self-reliant mutual aid might be applied to recycling activities (page 70). In most of these examples, links to the local community are more tenuous: local people may be workers or beneficiaries but not necessarily involved in project management. Groundwork Trusts and their projects were similarly imposed from outside originally, though all the Trusts are now moving towards greater community influence over their work. Ashram Acres seems to have made the transition from a 'professional' beginning to community control more rapidly than most (page 10).

● *Environmental enterprises.* Occasionally, initiatives start when 'environmental entrepreneurs' see 'green' business opportunities to be exploited, which also allow other goals to be pursued. Camden Garden Centre, for example, combines commercial objectives with those of job creation and training (page 75). Arboreta Papers, Blackwall Products and Paperback are all run as businesses but also aim to promote recycling (pages 22, 78, 80). Some small 'green' businesses have been spawned from existing environmental initiatives (like those of Avon FOE, page 18, and the UCAT enterprises, page 39).

INNOVATION

All the projects described in the case studies have been innovative. Although many of them could be said to have started out as local adaptations of ideas already tried elsewhere, all have been substantially modified to fit new circumstances. Although Windmill Hill City Farm used experience from Kentish Town, its emphasis upon developing community services based on the farm is new. UCAT's ideas for appropriate energy-saving technology in the city needed considerable adaptation of the pioneering work at the National Centre for Alternative Technology in Machynlleth.

Technically, many of the projects have been innovative, developing new practical approaches by experimenting – for example, with low-cost land management methods. Some projects have pioneered methods of community involvement in environmental action (those of Tower Hamlets Environment Trust, for example, page 96). Managerially too, some of the initiatives have been experimental, not only internally with their own organisation, but in learning to 'work the system', becoming skilled in negotiation and persuasion.

In almost all the projects studied, the energy, enthusiasm and persistence of two or three individuals with previous experience of the ideas (and usually specialist technical skills) were essential ingredients in getting projects started and sustaining them through initial negotiations. These pioneers – or community entrepreneurs – were often unemployed graduates and frequently seeking to apply their own skills in new directions. They have been opportunistic, risk-taking, experimental and imaginative with limited and disparate funds, sometimes showing considerable entrepreneurial flair. All the schemes relied heavily upon volunteers to get started; normally, it was at least a year before the projects had any paid staff.

STAGES OF DEVELOPMENT

Most of the schemes studied were helped with access to land: by peppercorn or low rents, usually from local authorities willing to let an experiment run for at least three years. It is doubtful if any of the projects could have survived without this help. Most have demonstrated sufficient success for arrangements to be renewed – though not without uncertainty and delays.

Acquiring premises has been more difficult, with less help offered. Those running projects have often found it hard to find accommodation in the desired location, of the right kind (many have specific requirements including the need for a large storage or working space). Although the premises eventually found were often subsidised (Ashram Acres and the Bristol Energy Centre, for example, used condemned council properties), most projects could have benefited from more help here – both at the start and later on, when new premises were needed.

Almost all the schemes had financial help in some form which allowed action on site to begin, although labour initially was volunteer. Environmental businesses used less conventional sources of support, including guaranteed loans, grants and the Enterprise Allowance Scheme. Projects were already running before MSC funding was secured.

Subsequent development is more varied: interesting patterns have taken place in different types of scheme. Each is, of course, unique, but there are some common experiences. Growth and diversification do not usually happen gradually but in bursts of activity, following a lull after the initial action. Early demonstration of 'something on the ground' was felt to be vital to acquire credibility with funders and other supporters and sustain community interest. Then groups consolidate their organisation and initial leaders may be replaced when the first paid staff are appointed. Even so, in most of the cases studied, the original leaders remained involved in some way. The more successful schemes, in terms of growth and diversification, are marked by a continuity of personnel.

Rapid expansion often comes with the first MSC team and this can pose difficult management problems for inexperienced, mainly volunteer, leaders. This is often a time for conflict – between staff and the management body, between staff and volunteers and among the paid staff, especially over the style of management. Indeed, some projects may collapse at this time, or split apart where there are major differences in goals and priorities. Internal management issues, with debates over co-operative or heirarchical styles, seem to dominate at this stage, with rather less emphasis upon executive action. Groups running some of the initiatives studied felt that expansion came too quickly: all the management time and energy was absorbed with new staff and day-to-day problems, leaving none for planning ahead.

ENVIRONMENTAL DEVELOPMENT AGENCIES

Among some of the more resilient and long-lived of the initiatives studied (those begun about 10 years ago), an interesting pattern of development has emerged – of an increasing number of interlinked activities all of which are in some way related to the environmental foundation of the project. Measured by their turnover, and numbers working (both paid and unpaid), these schemes have grown rapidly, not always in geographical area, but in the variety of related activities and objectives pursued. They have diversified from an environmental preoccupation into social and income-generating activities. This has happened partly as a response to a better perception of what the local needs are. But it is also a reaction to increasing financial pressure as early funding (given for an experimental period) diminishes and sustainability demands that schemes search for ways of supplementing grant income by selling products or services.

It is possible to see these 'compendium' schemes (Windmill Hill City Farm, the Bristol Energy Centre, Ashram Acres, Tower Hamlets Environment Trust and Avon FOE Ltd are all good examples) as 'environmentally-based development agencies', and three special features characterise their way of working. They are:

- environmentally opportunistic

- socially responsive

- economically innovative

Although the emphasis on each of these characteristics varies in different schemes, there are a number of common strengths associated with this multi-objective approach.

Environmental opportunism

The projects all make use of locally wasted assets – land, buildings, energy, refuse and people – to deliver practical environmental gains which would not otherwise have happened. The benefits, in terms of dereliction removed, trees planted, buildings restored and insulated have been substantial, sometimes beginning a transformation of run-down inner city neighbourhoods – as at Ashram Acres and Windmill Hill (pages 10 and 33). Visible transformations have been greatest with the greening schemes, but other projects have brought indirect environmental gains – in buildings renovated, litter cleared, refuse reduced, and sometimes in the intangible improvement of an area's image.

Most of the schemes are also used by their managing organisations as practical examples to promote environmental awareness, both among visitors on site and in the classroom with school children and adults. Some link the practical action closely to campaigning on environmental issues, as does Avon FOE.

A number of the schemes have been innovative technically, and have been successful in passing on their findings to local authorities who are beginning to adopt new methods of environmental management:

• Landlife projects and those of Tower Hamlets Environment Trust have pioneered the low-cost greening of small urban sites subject to vandalism, using ecological methods and community involvement.

• Ashram Acres and Windmill Hill City Farm are experimenting with more productive and environmentally benign means of producing food in the city, using a variety of organic growing methods.

• The Bristol Energy Centre has shown how energy-conserving measures can be combined to reduce fuel bills by adapting a small terraced house.

• Other local energy projects have tested a variety of insulation materials and devised 'best buys' as well as exploring energy information methods.

• Some of the local recycling schemes are devising new products from waste (see Blackwall Products and Paperback, pages 78 and 80).

Social responsiveness

What began as environmental initiatives have, in many cases, become important resources which meet the wider social needs of a locality. They do so in a variety of ways – providing play facilities for children or activities for women and the elderly, which reduce loneliness and develop skills. Some projects provide cheap goods such as recycled furniture for those who would otherwise go without them. Local energy schemes may have begun as examples of practical action on resource conservation but now deliver warmth cheaply for those on low incomes. They have come to represent a coalition of welfare, employment and environmental interests. And, like some of the other compendium schemes, they have become transfer points for meeting other needs – helping people with their access to benefits, house repairs and gardening or providing – if only temporarily – companionship for the lonely.

Most of these projects are constantly responding to new opportunities to meet needs otherwise unmet locally: Windmill Hill began a community bus when there was a problem with local public transport, CSAWS provided a sitting area for old people in its courtyard.

For some schemes, this responsiveness to social needs becomes a major objective, for others it happens incidentally.

Ventures like Ashram Acres and Windmill Hill play a vital part in sustaining a sense of community, hosting celebrations and many other events and becoming involved in local issues. Some groups, like Tower Hamlets Environment Trust, see the empowering of local people as a major objective of their work on environmental improvement. THET has been especially concerned to involve people at all stages of a project, devising ways of reaching different groups in the community (page 96).

All these projects have been successful in influencing local policy-making on social, environmental and economic issues. Ashram Acres, for example, convinced Birmingham City's Economic Development Unit that a job creation project based on vegetable growing should be mounted; UCAT through its work at the Bristol Energy Centre, has persuaded the City Council to prepare an energy plan for housing estates in the city; THET persuaded the London Borough of Tower Hamlets to organise a community gardening service and full consultations on its Inner Area Programme.

A major and developing social role of many of the initiatives studied (and especially the multi-objective, compendium schemes) is in providing work – unpaid and paid, temporary and permanent – in areas of generally high unemployment. All the projects have expanded their workforce, some substantially. They seem to be particularly effective at providing work for women, for ethnic minorities, disabled people and for other disadvantaged groups that may be considered harder-to-employ (see also chapter 5).

Training – both in life and technical skills – is an essential component of their work and considerable effort is devoted to increasing job satisfaction. Training and counselling in job-finding is often given and there seems to be a good record in finding permanent jobs for those on temporary work schemes and sometimes for volunteers (chapter 5).

In all these ways, protecting or improving environmental resources can be seen as a valuable initial focus which may trigger local action in ways that eventually bring many benefits. Some schemes, on the Sholver estate, for example, appear to be at the early stages of this process. Others studied, like Windmill Hill City Farm, would now not be described primarily as environmental initiatives; their social roles are dominant, although these all depend on the 'green' environment of the farm. Thus, the social advantages of environmentally-motivated projects, and the ways in which individuals gain from their participation in the work offered, may eventually outweigh the obvious environmental benefits of acres greened or trees planted or tonnes of refuse reclaimed. Their values cannot easily be measured in these terms.

Economic innovation

As initial grants have run out and funding has become less certain, many environmental schemes have had to try to become more financially self-supporting. They have become adept at pooling funds from many different sources and exploring ways of getting help in kind and scrounging low-cost materials.

Many projects are run by their organising groups on a shoestring. Although it is difficult to give hard evidence here, most of the initiatives studied appear to be delivering environmental gains at a lower cost than when equivalent work is done by other sectors: Landlife, for example, can reclaim wasteland for £6 per acre, a fraction of the usual cost to local authorities. On the schemes studied, wages and benefits were often less than equivalents in the public or private sectors.

Some environmental initiatives have spawned trading enterprises, selling environmental goods and services. There are few of them and they are usually small, but like other 'micro-firms' they have pioneered new markets with little help (this is discussed further in chapter 5).[17]

COMMUNITY BUSINESSES

These new enterprises may be run as independent businesses (although they differ from conventional firms). But sometimes, as at Windmill Hill, they remain under the wing of the parent initiative, and act as 'community businesses' returning some income to finance other non-profitable activities.

Community businesses have been variously defined and it is clear that the term is applied, somewhat loosely, to a whole range of ventures that try to blend social and economic objectives. Peter Kuenstler cites the definition:

. . . a trading organisation which is owned and controlled by the local community and which aims to create self-supporting and viable jobs for local people . . . and to use profits made from its business activities either to create more employment, or to provide local services, or to support local charitable work. A community business is likely to be a multi-purpose enterprise, and it may be based on a geographical community or a community of interest.[18]

Trevor Watling goes further to identify community businesses with a training objective and with services targetted at disadvantaged groups.[19] It is acknowledged that only some of these features may be present in any one enterprise: in a study of community businesses in London, Trevor Watling found that community control in terms of elected members on the board of management was particularly rare. And Andrew McArthur notes that community businesses often fail to live up to their ideals.[20]

On these definitions it is possible to see those compendium schemes that have trading elements as containing community businesses. What distinguishes them from enterprises discussed in other recent studies (including the London Survey) is their concern with the environmental as well as the social and economic ingredients of regeneration. Like the vegetable-growing project of Ashram Acres, they are pioneering an approach to greater local self-reliance whereby more of what is needed locally can be met from local resources.

DEVELOPMENT TRUSTS

In their blending of several objectives (environmental, social and economic), in their concern with the development of land and buildings, with community involvement and with the regeneration of an area wider than just one site, some of the 'environmental development agencies' studied here also qualify as 'development trusts' – a newly-defined type of organisation in which interest is growing and which is seen to offer certain advantages as an approach to urban regeneration. A recent DOE study defines them as follows:

Community-based development trusts are independent, not-for-profit organisations which bring together public, private and voluntary sectors to take action to renew an area physically, socially, economically and in spirit. They encourage substantial involvement by local people and aim to sustain their operations at least in part by generating revenue.[21]

On this definition, Tower Hamlets Environment Trust, Windmill Hill City Farm and the Urban Centre for Appropriate Technology would seem to be examples of environmentally-motivated development trusts – although they are not all legally constituted as trusts.

SUMMING UP THE STRENGTHS

A general point to emerge from the environmental initiatives studied, especially the multi-objective schemes, is that the sum is greater than the parts. These initiatives are integrative, linking traditionally separate areas of activity (environment and business have been seen as opposed) and blending objectives in synergistic ways so that each benefits from work on the others. The projects have welcomed the challenge to respond to local needs and have explored imaginatively the social and economic dimensions of environmental action.

The initiatives all remain small and flexible enough to do this. They rarely have more than 10 full-time staff, often fewer than six. Local authorities, with many large, centralised departments, even if they aim to link action on the ground, find it difficult to do so, unless departments are devolved to neighbourhood level. Even then, action is most often bound by traditional professional and bureaucratic boundaries.

The compendium schemes studied reflect more closely people's perception of what makes up their local environment – that it is about how it looks and feels and works for them, about social contact, having fun, and is – ideally – adaptable to their needs and to opportunities that arise. In many of the schemes studied, problems are seen as solutions in disguise, liabilities are turned into assets, 'externalities' become the major theme. And the *process* of environmental action is seen to be as important as the *product*, sometimes more so. Creating, managing and celebrating a greenspace, recycling wastes or insulating homes become valuable activities in their own right, which can provide satisfying work, self-esteem, skills and social contact. Some of the projects studied have had as healing and therapeutic effect upon a whole neighbourhood as they have for individuals. (Ashram Acres, Windmill Hill, and Sholver, pages 10, 33 and 51).

While a high quality or high volume end-product is or should be aimed for (and is vital if voluntary sector projects are to dispel an amateur image and build up credibility), this may be of less concern than the quality of the participatory experience – for clients or workers. It becomes important, therefore, to ensure projects continue to offer new tasks and new challenges to be tackled – that they remain unfinished, constantly adapting to local circumstances.

In all these ways, the multi-objective initiatives studied reflect a dynamic, holistic approach, fundamentally different from the traditional, static view (common in both the public and private sectors) of the urban environment as a by-product of, and backdrop to, other activities, or one in which the aim is to achieve 'finished' improvements of a standard, conventional kind. This is a unique style of working with strengths that are not easily replicated in the public or private sectors even if financial circumstances change. It suggests that voluntary sector environmental initiatives have a permanent rather than a temporary role to play.

But this is not an easy way of working. Because of their multiple objectives, schemes have become inventive at packaging funds from different sources but have fallen at the margins of interest for most funding organisations who look to support projects with a clear central theme. And combining objectives in one scheme brings internal conflicts. Being flexible and responsive in community terms should not be an excuse for shoddy work or poor business management. Chapter 6 looks at some of these problems; the next two chapters consider issues of work creation.

Windmill Hill City Farm

4 Bristol children at Windmill Hill City Farm.

Windmill Hill, one of the earliest city farms in Britain, lies on 4½ acres of land, which was once a scrap yard, in Bedminster, south Bristol. In 10 years, the farm has transformed the neighbourhood, from a landscape of rubble and abandoned cars to a thriving community centre used and valued by thousands of local people.

In the spring of 1976, a group of local residents, led by Mike and Dawn Primarolo, objected to Bristol City Council's proposal to use the site (which the council owned) as a high security lorry park. At a popular event organised to gauge local opinion on what should happen, the idea of a city farm emerged and the council agreed to lease the land at a peppercorn rent for five years. Volunteers began work in 1977, clearing the site, renovating a derelict building (to provide workshop and meeting space) and establishing the farmyard. The first management committee was formed with local people and the farm was registered as a charity. It began to raise funds from trusts and local companies and canvassed for donations of materials to use on the site.

Responding to the needs of the locality, the farm started the first of its many community activities – a summer playscheme for local children. Later in the same year, the farm took a lead in organising a community bus service in partnership with local councils and a bus company. Residents had been told that it was not possible to provide a normal service on the steep and narrow streets of Windmill Hill.

The layout of the farm and its activities have developed over a decade of response to community need. The aim is to 'provide a wide range of educational and recreational facilities for all groups in the community, and at the same time create an attractive, useful and productive environment'. Thus the farm combines environmental and economic goals with its essential community purpose.

The site now has six main activity areas: the farmyard; community gardens; paddocks for grazing animals; a chicken tractor system (for egg production); an all-weather sports pitch and associated play spaces; and a nature reserve. The farm is continually adapting to new demands: accessible gardens for disabled and elderly people are a recent development; there are herb and butterfly gardens and a tree nursery is under construction. Wherever possible, planting on the farm is designed for visual improvement and to serve other purposes, for example, as animal feed, for composting, dyeing and craftwork.

Around the farmyard is a complex of buildings housing farm animals, the playcentre, workshop, craft and administration space, a café and dairy. Some buildings, like the playcentre and the café, have been purpose-built, but throughout the development of the farm, an effort has been made to acquire buildings cheaply. A barn was partly designed and built by architectural students, and completed – at a total cost of £20 – by volunteers. The 'rumpus' playroom is an old school classroom; most of its equipment was constructed by mothers of children using the playcentre: the total cost of the building and its contents was £3,700. Unwanted but usable building materials (such as bricks) are collected from a variety of local sources and stored in a recycling yard on the farm, and there is now a 'recycling trail' showing where reclaimed materials have been used.

How it works

In an area of high unemployment with few other community facilities (especially for mothers with young children) the farm offers something for everyone. A playcentre operates throughout the week, with sessions for pre-schoolers and the handicapped. Latest attractions, enjoyed especially by handicapped children, are a computer and the popular 'rumpus room' – a maze of soft, safe foam shapes. Childrens' clubs are organised after school and on Saturday mornings, all based on farm activities. There is a supervised adventure playground for older children and an all-weather sports pitch for teenagers and adults, with changing rooms.

A number of the farm's activities make up a programme of

'community care'. There are support groups for new parents and those with handicapped children, both meeting weekly. A variety of courses are included in the Women's Health Project, with educational and exercise classes and a discussion group on mental health. Long-stay patients from a psychiatric hospital come regularly to work in the gardens, the workshops and help with the farm animals. Others also come to the farm to take part in these activities as part of their training or work experience. There are counselling groups for young people who may have problems, and senior citizens meet weekly at the farm to enjoy a chat or try some craft activity.

Among the farm's most attractive features are the small community gardens, let first to those who live in nearby flats, but also used by physically and mentally handicapped visitors. A large greenhouse extends the possibilities for horticultural therapy and a variety of training programmes and provides plants to stock the gardens and for sale. Here, and in the gardens, there is experiment and research on growing and composting methods.

The farm responds especially well to the needs of women for sociable and creative activity. As well as learning animal husbandry, horticultural and food-processing skills, they can take printing, spinning, weaving and other craft courses or make and repair furniture in a community workshop, which provides tools and guidance for woodwork.

One, sometimes two, schools visit each day, are shown around by farm staff and can work in the education room. There are 'educational days' linked to farm activities and special visits are arranged for deaf, blind and other handicapped children. Future plans include further development of the sports facilities, a building for the community care activities and to serve as a base for volunteers, and the linkage of Windmill Hill with a commercially viable organic farm outside Bristol.

Volunteers created and in large measure sustain Windmill Hill – some 500 are associated with the farm. They serve on the Management Committee and Area Management Teams, and work alongside paid staff on practical tasks. Many of the core staff and MSC team began by volunteering. 'I started coming' says one YTS trainee 'when I was seven. Now the farm is my second home.'

Most volunteers are local, both men and women, from all social groups. They come for different reasons: some are looking for paid work and feel that volunteering provides useful experience, others want to work with the animals or seek companionship with people. In addition to these are the 'placement' volunteers – those on work experience, training courses or at the farm for therapeutic reasons. The community care activities are an important focus for volunteer activity (helping with the senior citizens group, for example). And volunteers are often pioneers: indeed some farm activities (such as the drama club) would not take place without them.

There is a part-time volunteer organiser, funded by the MSC and based at the farm at weekends and for two midweek days. The aim is to provide good volunteer experiences and get extra work done in ways that complement the paid staff. The organiser negotiates with them to find appropriate work for volunteers and supervises their activities and welfare, trying to make use of special skills and accommodate special needs. 'Timetabled' volunteers are especially encouraged – those who will work regularly each week, fortnight or month; they receive expenses and lunch (depending on their hours). Every day the farm will have at least two volunteers at work, during the summer playschemes there may be 20–30 each day. Volunteers and paid staff alike enjoy frequent social events, advice on welfare benefits and help in searching for jobs.

The farm benefits now, as at the beginning, from the driving force of committed volunteers like Mike Primarolo and Lin Whitfield, both of whom work at the National Federation of City Farms which has its offices in the neighbourhood.

Funding and management
In 1978, an Urban Aid grant paid for a full-time farmer, a workshop organiser and an administrator (both part-time) and provided £3,000 of capital to establish the farm. In 1983, a further Urban Aid grant of £43,000 was awarded over three years to cover building materials and equipment. Bristol City Council continues to let the site at a peppercorn rent and provides grant aid towards staff costs (£7,850 in 1984/85, £12,000 in 1985/86 and £28,000 in 1986/87). The Bristol City Council contribution will decrease steadily in forthcoming years as the farm's community businesses increase their revenue. Avon County Council (formerly with the Area Health Authority) pays for staff members to organise a variety of community care activities, including work with mentally disturbed patients in the gardens, and with the elderly (£12,600 in 1986).

The farm now employs 19 on permanent jobs (8 posts are fulltime, the rest are job-shares). Half of these are presently supported from the farm's own revenue (£44,000 in 1986/87) made up of fees from a membership of over 700 families, from the weekly activities and courses, the sale of farm produce, local fund raising and gifts. Links with local firms are strong: the farm benefits from favourable prices and donations of goods – most recently of waste from wholefood shops which cuts the high cost of feeding animals. Where possible supplies are bought locally and from new enterprises in the community.

Since the early days, the Manpower Services Commission has funded a number of job creation programmes, and presently supports a 50-place Community Programme scheme to help run the farm, its caring activities and carry out building work. The farm's annual budget (excluding the MSC scheme) is some £100,000. The

aim is to offer more services and develop more community businesses (like the café) and so become increasingly self-supporting
with less reliance on short-term funding.

The management style is non-hierarchical with no overall director. A wide variety of local people serve on the Management Committee (elected from the membership) and on seven Area Management Teams through which the farm's different users organise their
activities (each team including a member of the Management
Committee). There are sub-committees for finance and personnel,
and support groups on events and publicity.

There is much emphasis on training for staff and volunteers,
including induction courses, first aid, training in management (with
the regular help of a consultant), assertiveness, and special skills
such as carpentry and animal husbandry. Many technical courses
are organised by the National Federation of City Farms and some
take place at Windmill Hill.

Good links have already been established with a network of
European urban farms, youth exchanges have taken place with one
farm in Germany – and more are planned in other EEC countries.

Windmill Hill is a working model of community resourcefulness.
It makes productive use of wasteland, creates a green oasis in the
city, offers recreational and educational experiences for all ages and
is reaching out in an innovative way to realise the opportunities for
community gain. 'Local people' says Lucy English, current
chairman of the Management Committee, 'joined together to create
the farm on a derelict site deep in refuse, rubble and rats. We
survived the early years of uncertainty and setbacks. We can now
look forward to a self-sufficient and expanding future.'

Bristol Energy Centre

5 The low energy house in Bedminster where energy-saving features are demonstrated.

In Bedminster, a low-income district of Bristol, the Urban Centre for Appropriate Technology has created a unique initiative incorporating three mutually supporting activities. A small terraced property, typical of the neighbourhood, has been adapted as a 'low energy house' demonstrating many energy-saving features. This is the base for a local insulation and energy advice team: BEAT. Nearby, a further house has been converted as a community energy workshop offering a variety of training courses. The Bristol Energy Centre supports 5 full-time and 16 MSC-funded employees.

The Urban Centre for Appropriate Technology (UCAT) was set up in Bristol by three people, two of whom had worked with the National Centre for Alternative Technology (NCAT) in Machynlleth, Wales. The intention was to adapt what had been learnt in Wales to provide a demonstration of resource-saving methods that were appropriate to the city. Social ideals of co-operative working were also important.

UCAT was established in 1979 under the wing of the Society for Environmental Improvement – a registered charity. By 1987,

UCAT had spawned not only the Bristol Energy Centre but a number of independent enterprises, including:

- the Green Leaf Bookshop, selling environmental and related materials and providing work for four

- the wholefood Green Leaf Cafe run, since 1985, as a co-op now providing work for four

- Green Leaf Builders – a design and build co-op now providing work for six

- Greens and Beans – a wholefood retailing co-op of four

- Low Energy Supply Systems – a two-man UCAT trading company selling and installing low energy equipment

UCAT's initiatives, including those that became the Bristol Energy Centre in 1986, all began with volunteers. Two people (Hugh Barton and Nigel Heggie) were initially funded as part-time co-ordinators by the Joseph Rowntree Charitable Trust and the first MSC Community Programme began in 1983. Other grants for UCAT's programme have come from the Gulbenkian Foundation, Tudor Trust and other charities. The small businesses have been developed, mainly since 1982, often by people following up their MSC CP experience. Most are now self-funded. Volunteers played an important part in UCAT's development – about 30 were regular participants in the early years.

Low energy house
In 1981, Bristol City Council offered UCAT the use of condemned properties in Philip Street, Bedminster, at a peppercorn rent for five years. Work began on the conversion of one of the Victorian two-bedroomed properties, incorporating and describing a large number of low-cost energy-saving measures: double and triple glazing, passive and active solar heating, cavity wall insulation and draught-proofing. Some equipment was given by insulation firms; some was experimental and built by UCAT members. Volunteers have played a significant role, both in the renovation and manning of the house to give free energy advice.

The modifications have brought substantial energy savings: a boiler one third of the size normally required for such a house is used, and heating bills are down by 60 per cent. The kitchen was built to minimise energy use and encourage waste recycling; the garden is designed for organic cultivation, with an energy-saving greenhouse.

Although it took considerably longer than planned, work on the house was largely complete when it was officially opened in September 1985. Until that time, casual visitors and school parties came intermittently for energy information. After the opening, publicity on local radio and television brought more inquiries and 2,000 visitors over the next year. The low energy house now deals with some 200 queries each month but its value is more as a teaching resource to support the training and education programme than as a visitor centre.

During the renovation phase, 23 were employed on the Community Programme. The demonstration house is now run by 8 of the Energy Centre's total of 16 CP staff – 4 energy advisers, 2 gardeners, an administrator and a publicity officer.

Energy Action Teams

By 1986 UCAT was sponsoring three insulation teams: two in Bristol and one in Bath (jointly sponsored with Bath City Council). In keeping with UCAT's philosophy of devolving responsibility to small groups, the Bath team and one of the Bristol teams are now sponsored by other voluntary organisations in the area in which they operate. The Bristol Energy Action Team (BEAT), with 8 MSC workers, is co-ordinated from an office beside the low energy house.

The Bristol Energy Centre, through BEAT, advises and trains other local energy projects and draught-proofs some 50 homes a month for low-income families in Bristol. Follow-up calls are made to all the homes insulated so that the work can be checked and further advice can be offered on energy saving, heating allowances and other benefits.

Community Energy Workshop

Close to the low energy house, another condemned terraced property has been renovated as an energy workshop with funding from Bristol City Council's Employment Initiatives Unit and the Gulbenkian Foundation. With a full-time manager (initially funded by Bristol City Council), the workshop offers space, tools and tuition for a variety of building and repair jobs. Training is a major activity. A number of courses and trips are run, intended for working professionals (including local authority and housing association staff), for unemployed people and those on the Community Programme (who are financed by the MSC's Avon Training Agency) and for schools. The courses are designed partly in response to community requests; they teach practical skills of construction, repair and maintenance, such as the use of tools, woodwork, plumbing, insulation and bicycle repair. Even so, the emphasis is upon energy topics. The workshop offers courses on 'energy awareness' for housing officers and several courses have been planned with Neighbourhood Energy Action for members of local energy projects: including 'energy advice' and 'condensation and ventilation'. Participants can be trained and tested for the City and Guilds Certificate in Draught-proofing.

People who want to use the energy workshop facilities pay an annual membership subscription and a session fee of 75p. With the income from course fees and membership, the workshop can support a full-time co-ordinator for the Energy Centre and contributes to the funding of three other posts.

Linked to the workshop is a low-cost energy advisory service for community groups and small businesses, and it is planned to upgrade the technical consultancy offered to the Council Housing Department and housing associations. In the latest initiative, Bristol Energy Centre (with support from the City Council) has joined forces with a local architectural co-operative to offer a low energy, self-build housing service to help unemployed people build energy efficient homes cheaply.

Other projects have grown out of work at the Centre at various times – though not all have survived. 'Windcheaters' began in 1985 when two of BEAT's Community Programme workers set up a small draught-proofing business on the Enterprise Allowance scheme, using the skills learnt on their MSC year. They worked part-time and continued trading for two years, but limited publicity and problems with marketing have forced the business to close. There was no feasibility study, and no specialist business advice available, either locally or nationally, tailored to their enterprise: help with pricing and marketing was felt to be especially needed.

The Bristol Energy Centre has close links with many other voluntary organisations, including Shelter, Age Concern, housing associations, tenants' groups, schools and with the neighbouring Windmill Hill City Farm (page 33), especially over publicity and the use of each others' services. The Centre and Avon Friends of the Earth Energy Services (page 22) jointly promote their activities and help each other with referrals.

One of UCAT's aims is to improve energy efficiency throughout Bristol: BEAT have estimated that a third of the council properties in the city (some 15,000 homes) need basic insulation. In 1985, UCAT persuaded the City Council to sponsor a conference of tenants' groups and many other agencies concerned about fuel poverty. Subsequently, a pressure group, Bristol Tenants for Fuel Economy, was formed: the council established a Housing Energy Working Party to advise its Housing Committee and is considering the appointment of an energy advice co-ordinator. The Energy Workshop has devised a training programme for council staff and Hugh Barton, of UCAT, prepared a comprehensive energy plan for the city concentrating on public housing estates. Now, the national Energy Efficiency Office is grant aiding the Centre to run a major local campaign on energy saving.

Management

The Urban Centre for Appropriate Technology is organised collectively through a 'moot' which represents all the separate initiatives, and charitable status, independent of the Society for Environmental Improvement, is being sought. Fine tuning the way this decision-making body operates is a perennial issue. The Energy Centre is managed by the core group of five permanent staff, consulting with the MSC staff. Considerable effort is devoted, collectively, to improving job satisfaction.

MSC programmes have been a mixed blessing – providing a much-needed workforce but one in which the commitment of individuals to UCAT's ideals has varied. Early on, the constantly changing workforce was demanding of management resources which could not always be mustered with a small core of permanent staff. Enlisting commitment to a long-term aim from those whose jobs are part-time and highly temporary has been no less of a problem here than on other projects. At times, integrating one-year MSC workers into the co-operative style of UCAT's management and working proved difficult. Now that more staff have permanent jobs, long-term planning can resume.

While UCAT has developed with a clear focus on energy-saving, it has spawned a number of linked but independent projects on a wide range of environmental issues – most concerned with a practical approach to living resourcefully in the city. In these small and mutually supportive groups, UCAT has pioneered a collective way of working. There is much exchange of ideas, services and volunteer effort between the projects; many participants are enthusiastic and dedicated. Some MSC staff were volunteers first, and others have stayed on as volunteers after their one year on the Community Programme.

Energy conservation remains an important theme in UCAT's work and it is largely through the experience of the Bristol Energy Centre operations that UCAT is beginning to influence the local authority and play an increasing role in the community. 'Our message', says Jenny Hendy of the Energy Centre, 'is about much more than hayboxes and woolly hats'. Overall, the approach is less overtly 'alternative', more appropriate and feasible for urban people to adopt than many of the ideas pioneered by the parent organisation, NCAT, in Wales. Some UCAT participants have criticised the attempt to influence people as too low key and piously hopeful. And it is clear that internal management issues and the continual search for funds have occupied much time and energy. But these are common problems for young schemes.

Among its successes, UCAT can count the refurbishment of several derelict buildings and the basic insulation of 3,000 homes. Indirectly UCAT has created more than 20 permanent jobs in six new enterprises, provides temporary work for 16, skills training, advice and is beginning to influence local policies. It illustrates how effective a voluntary organisation can be in providing inspiration and co-ordination on *practical* approaches to energy efficiency. 'And this', argues Hugh Barton, one of the founders, 'is a crucial element in building a more conserving, sustainable society.'

4 Making the Most of Volunteering

In all the initiatives studied, volunteers have played a crucial role, especially at the start. Most projects only began because of the ideas, energies and persistence of volunteers. For some, like Ashram Acres and the Sholver Rangers, volunteers remain the major force for action.

At national level, a Volunteer Centre survey confirmed that volunteering mainly attracts people in the higher socio-economic groups and those in paid work.[22] David Gerard showed it to be associated with middle age, with middle-class status, extended education, and a family context with school-age children.[23] But it is difficult to generalise about who volunteers for environmental activity in the city: the national surveys are inconclusive and the case studies show that all ages are represented, working-class and middle-class people volunteer, although more men than women do so.

The motivations seem to be more varied than among those who volunteer for environmental work in the countryside.[24] For the volunteers interviewed in this study, social issues were as important as environmental ones, if not more so: volunteering was a way of bringing local benefits. Personal gains seem to be similar to those associated with other kinds of volunteering: it allows special interests and skills to be pursued, it increases self-esteem, combats isolation and promotes friendship. And environmental work can give much of the experience and disciplines of paid employment; volunteering can provide valuable training in social and technical skills which may help job-seekers to secure paid employment.

The case studies show that projects can benefit in a number of ways: volunteers (because of their freedom from outside control) can be especially valuable in stimulating further participation and building up a project's identity in the community. Local involvement reduces vandalism and can inform and help a community in other ways. On the Sholver Estate, young people acting as rangers have reduced the scale of damage done to homes, cared for older people and encouraged beneficial social exchange among residents (page 51). A special feature of environmental work is its attractiveness for whole families to volunteer, as at Ashram Acres (page 10).

But there are weaknesses and dangers when volunteering becomes a cheap substitute for paid work and the answer to public cuts in services. There is scope for people to be exploited and denied income. Projects may not provide worthwhile training or help for volunteers in finding paid work. Environmental improvement may also suffer: the quality of work done can be more difficult to control; volunteer effort, with its uncertainty over who and how many will turn out, is often difficult and time-consuming to organise. It may be tricky to manage volunteers alongside paid workers, needed skills may not exist and volunteers may require extensive and costly training which can divert paid staff from other essential project work.

The better schemes have overcome many of these problems. They combine paid and voluntary work and have trained managers for this. They discuss potential conflicts of interest in advance with unions, and make special arrangements to organise and motivate volunteers – for they believe that improving the 'volunteering experience' is at least as important a task as using volunteers for cheap or free extra manpower – an issue on which the Volunteer Centre, volunteer bureaux and others have devoted much campaigning effort.[25] The suggestion is that attitudes and practices have progressed faster in the social services, more slowly in environmental projects – urban and rural – where the perception of 'volunteers as manpower' lingers on. The organisers of a number of the schemes featured in this study felt that the status and support for volunteers must be improved, with more attention to ways of recognising and rewarding their contribution. The following conclusions have been distilled from the case studies where volunteering is significant.

INITIATING THE ACTION

Even where good ideas are generated locally, by committed people, this is seldom enough to get a scheme started and sustained. At least one person in the relevant local authority needs to be closely identified with an incipient project, providing a contact point for negotiating support, helping with access to land, buildings and funds, and showing continuing enthusiasm. Some local authorities have appointed community development officers and earmarked monies to support voluntary effort, as Manchester City Council has done in its Community Initiatives Fund. But few councils have any corporate policy towards volunteers. A number of the case studies show how valuable can be the role of community technical aid centres and other 'enabling' organisations (such as the Oldham and Rochdale Groundwork Trust at Sholver, the Free Form Arts Trust at Hackney Grove Garden and on the Provost estate, and Tower Hamlets Environment Trust) in mediating between volunteer groups and local authorities.[26]

The process of enlisting volunteers is usually slow and requires special effort in publicity and campaigning. It works best in those

localities and projects where potential volunteers can see the immediate benefits to themselves and where there are natural leaders who
can motivate local people. These 'animateurs'– originating locally or
brought in – are a vital means of identifying project opportunities,
defining tasks, mediating between different groups, and conducting
negotiations about funding or access with statutory and other
bodies. It is often possible to identify suitable animateurs from
established local groups who can be persuaded to take on environmental work. Local clubs, civic societies, companies, schools and
tenants' associations are all good places for recruiting volunteers.

Publicity to attract them seems to be most effective when it
concentrates upon the volunteer experience being offered rather
than on the need for free labour – especially in areas where there is
little or no tradition of self-help. It is useful to have specialist
training in publicity methods and creating good media relations and
there should be adequate project funds to do this well. Again, the
case studies show that 'enabling' organisations can be especially
helpful at the early project stage, arranging and following up a first
public meeting, identifying and synthesising needs, curbing unreal
expectations as well as providing technical advice. Celebrations can
be useful ways of attracting and keeping volunteers.

Volunteer bureaux and councils for voluntary service are already
active in directing volunteers towards environmental work, particularly in the countryside. There is room for them to play a greater role
in directing volunteers to urban schemes, and attracting new rec-
ruits to volunteering such as retired or soon-to-retire businessmen
whose managerial skills and hobby enthusiasms (natural history, for
example) can be very valuable in environmental work. Other
advantages – for example in the management and training of
volunteers – could also flow from a closer liaison between environmental organisations and local agencies like the councils for voluntary service.

KEEPING VOLUNTEERS HAPPY

Once a project has begun, its volunteers are not usually self-
organising but require management and care which attend as much
to their personal and social needs as to the development of their
technical skills. Volunteers need to feel that they are making a valid
contribution and are worthwhile members of the whole project
team, neither inferior nor dispensable. Most (though not all) like to
be involved in key decisions and the opportunity should be available
to help with administration, for this is one way of building up
identity with a project. A policy of 'equal opportunities' should
apply: indeed some environmental projects actively seek to involve
disadvantaged groups such as the disabled and ethnic minorities.
Regular volunteers, like paid staff members, should enjoy similar

training opportunities, insurance and advice on health and safety, first aid and vehicle and tool use. The Volunteer Centre, and most of those consulted on the case studies, argue that expenses should always be offered. And there are many non-monetary ways of recognising volunteer effort: appreciation needs to be frequently expressed, and there can be special awards and celebrations.

A number of case studies show the value of having a paid staff member to co-ordinate volunteers and sustain their motivation in these ways. This person needs considerable managerial and counselling skills to make the most of both a volunteer's experience and capacities and sometimes to act as his or her advocate. Special social skills and training will be required for work with particular kinds of volunteer: children and young people, disabled and unemployed people and those from ethnic minorities. Different groups sometimes do mix happily – Ashram Acres shows that it is possible for people with very different cultural backgrounds to work together.

The decision to volunteer is often closely linked to particular kinds of personal circumstance such as redundancy, bereavement and loneliness: co-ordinators must be prepared for situations that require skilful counselling. And they may have to get potentially conflicting groups – past and present volunteers, infrequent and regular ones, old and young, for example – to work together. For all these reasons, continuity in the co-ordinator post is important (and on job creation programmes, it is desirable to extend the normal one-year appointment). Beneficial arrangements can be made with local businesses to second or sponsor volunteer co-ordinators.

Social interaction is a major attraction for volunteers, but this too benefits from careful management. Environmental projects need a 'volunteer base' for meeting and refreshment, and the organisation of social and leisure events which can cement friendships and build up project identity.

Where environmental initiatives have become a valuable focus for community activity, it is important to 'design in' new opportunities for voluntary effort, after the pioneering phase. This means that a successful project may never finish – new tasks and new challenges continually arise around which fund raising, practical work and celebrations can take place. Local animateurs and enabling organisations may need to play a role here, alerting projects to new ideas and the possibilities for development, showing how some tasks can be followed up.

Volunteer co-ordinators need to be sensitive to patterns of free time in a neighbourhood so that no one is excluded because of his or her working schedule. Some groups can volunteer mid-week but opportunities (and co-ordinators) need to be available at weekends, after school and during school holidays as they are at Windmill Hill City Farm. And projects may have to cater for special needs to attract some volunteers – providing a crèche, for example. Management is easier where volunteers can be persuaded to commit themselves to a regular weekly period of work.

Selecting appropriate tasks is a crucial job for volunteer coordinators who must match the work that needs to be done to the different volunteers available. Advance negotiation with paid staff can often identify appropriate tasks but care is needed to fashion jobs to fit particular skills and personalities. In general, tasks for volunteers should offer variety and companionship, and quick results of obvious local benefit.

The Volunteer Centre suggests (and case studies confirm) that it is not possible to make a rigid distinction between tasks proper to volunteers and those for paid workers: arrangements have to suit specific circumstances. But organisers have to be sensitive to possible conflicts and negotiate early and fully with unions and professional associations where appropriate. The Volunteer Centre's 'Drain Guidelines' still provide a useful basis for negotiation.[27]

Working with volunteers is always uncertain; expectations and job planning have to be correspondingly flexible to accommodate few or many workers and different levels of skill.[28] For some projects, especially those concerned with greening, it is often hard to get volunteers for the day-to-day management jobs. Clearing litter, maintaining access, managing vegetation and repairing after vandalism can be unrewarding and repetitive tasks compared with the creative pioneering work. Some projects, like Hackney Grove Garden, have tackled this by designing for low maintenance, and by appointing a user committee and a key worker to take responsibility for daily management and organise volunteer 'work ins'.[29]

Deploying volunteers is never cost-free. Money must be spent on transport, materials, insurance, administration and individual out-of-pocket expenses. Among those concerned with the working conditions of volunteers, the feeling is that people who do unpaid environmental work are not reimbursed for their expenses often enough. Even where payments are available, claiming them may not be encouraged; and rates are lower than is usual for social service volunteering. One reason is that much environmental volunteering has traditionally taken place in the countryside and among people who have not claimed expenses. But environmental action in the city is attracting a wider range of volunteers, and it seems likely that free transport and payment of expenses (and provision of suitable clothing, footware and equipment) will become necessary prerequisites for volunteering.

VOLUNTEERING AND UNEMPLOYMENT

It might be thought that volunteering could offer unemployed people a way of meeting some of their needs – for improved self-esteem and social contact and the possibility of training that may improve job prospects. Some of the case studies do have unemployed volunteers who take this view and some unemployed volunteers on environmental projects do secure places subsequently on temporary work schemes and in permanent posts. On a few projects there is a migration of the same people from volunteering into temporary work schemes and back to volunteering again.

Yet, in practice, most environmental volunteering is done by those already in paid work. Research by volunteer bureaux in Britain estimates that the extent of all volunteering by the unemployed (10 per cent) is lower than that for the rest of the population (18 per cent).[30] The case studies show that it is not easy to attract or keep unemployed volunteers. Perhaps people in work are more likely to know of the opportunities, are less inhibited in their participation, and more receptive to the personal benefits.

Some of the supposed values of volunteering for unemployed people appear to be more theoretical than real. Stubbings, for example, argues that for those out of work, the choice of alternative activity is severely limited, not least by poverty.[31] Bishop shows that unemployed people enjoy fewer leisure activities; even volunteering may be too expensive when there are chances to earn money informally.[32] Moreover, the promotion of volunteering is weak compared with that of commercial leisure opportunities. And voluntary work, because of its association with professional groups, may appear an unattractive option particularly among those who are neither white nor middle class. Evaluations of volunteer programmes have found that unemployed people prefer to learn new skills in their free time.

The Voluntary Projects Programme is a special Manpower Services Commission (MSC) scheme designed to encourage unemployed people to volunteer for community projects (participants do not have to be registered as unemployed, and those that are can continue to claim benefit). Sponsors – in statutory or voluntary agencies – are financially supported to organise the volunteering and the emphasis is placed upon achieving a good and valuable experience for the volunteer with training in useful skills. In 1985, the VPP budget was £13.5 million; in 1987 it was £12 million covering 380 schemes. By MSC standards, this is a small programme and only 10 per cent of the VPP schemes are entirely or partly environmental. This limited number means that some applications for VPP places on environmental projects have been refused. Yet evaluations of the VPP show that, in terms of volunteer experience, it is a successful programme, its participants report a high level of satisfaction (although they are untypical of unemployed people, being younger, jobless for longer, less skilled and more often women).[33] Some volunteer organisers consulted in this study argue that the VPP is a valuable way of involving people in enjoyable environmental work who have few other chances to participate: they may, for example, be physically or mentally handicapped. With its emphasis upon volunteer co-ordination and training, the VPP has advantages over the Community Programme (see chapter 5) and seems worth expanding – not as a substitute for employment, but as an alternative to unemployment, and to help in the transition to paid work.

Managing environmental work with unemployed volunteers is likely to pose special problems. Participants will often have low self-esteem; indeed, the higher incidence of depression and poor health among the unemployed may mean that volunteers need more help than they are able to give. Timekeeping can be poor and there is likely to be considerable uncertainty over who will turn up. The more committed and skilled volunteers will leave as they find paid work, so projects must constantly recruit new volunteers. Some trades unions, local authorities and professional groups dislike MSC programmes like the VPP and the potential competition they bring; their co-operation over environmental projects may be refused.

The case studies where unemployed people have been involved as volunteers suggest that the ingredients for success include:

- having a sympathetic and specially trained co-ordinator

- selecting relevant tasks that provide useful skills training and, as at Ashram Acres, obvious personal benefits

- keeping the identity of the volunteer projects clear and separate from other projects

- providing expenses and clothing

- giving advice on financial benefits and how to claim them

- providing help in job searching and where possible, encouraging a transition to permanent paid work

- organising social and leisure events, including, where possible, volunteer holidays away from the home base

JOB CREATION AND VOLUNTEERING

The case studies show that many environmental projects initiated by voluntary action can generate paid work – both temporary and permanent. In a number of cases, volunteers have moved on to temporary work schemes and sometimes new businesses. And MSC teams can be a training ground for new volunteers.

But there is also evidence that temporary work schemes can

depress opportunities for volunteering. The more experienced and active volunteers may be attracted into MSC schemes which fill an area of voluntary work but leave a gap later. Volunteer morale may fall when it is realised others are being paid for the same task and the quality of work done may decline. A project's goals and autonomy can suffer, and there are problems of staff and financial insecurity – discussed in the next chapter.[34]

There is some evidence that organisations which expand very quickly, by taking on large MSC temporary employment schemes, find that their management resources rapidly become overstretched. Preoccupied with organising paid workers, managers have little time left to devote to volunteers. And when these are greatly outnumbered by paid workers on a project, then there is little opportunity of retaining a sense of shared participation and responsibility – and a danger that local responsiveness will be lost. In general it seems that where volunteers and paid employees are to work together, numbers need to be comparable and management time shared.

The present pressure on voluntary agencies to sponsor more and larger temporary work schemes (increased with the launch of UK 2000) will mean a continued colonisation of opportunities for voluntary work, unless, overall, more environmental work can be generated, adequate management resources are provided, and there is sufficient goodwill to negotiate different territories and maximise the advantages of linking paid and unpaid work.

Sholver Rangers

6 Tim Edge and two of the Sholver Rangers planting bulbs.

Sholver is a housing estate, set on a bleak and windswept hillside overlooking Oldham, an industrial town in North West England. The estate, of some 5,000 housing units, was built in the 1960s to take overspill families from the city. But may of the houses have been gutted by fire and boarded up. Vandalism and flytipping are commonplace and there are numerous and severe social problems – of high unemployment (especially among school-leavers), drug abuse, teenage pregnancy and truancy. The 'image' of Sholver – among residents and in the local press – is very poor. The environment, likewise, is shabby and unkempt – with large areas of monotonous grassland, damaged trees and litter blowing about.

The estate overlooks the Beal Valley, which has all the classic problems of an urban fringe landscape on the edge of a decaying industrial area, with vandalism and trespass affecting local farms. The Beal Valley Project of the Oldham and Rochdale Groundwork Trust is designed to bring together land use interests to work out and implement a management strategy for the area, improving both the visual landscape and opportunities for outdoor recreation.

In 1984, a local resident of Sholver, Martyn Atkinson – an unemployed ambulance driver – worked voluntarily with a group of residents and their children to make some improvements to a corner of the estate which was threatened with demolition. Calling them-selves the Rembrandt Walk and Titian Rise Residents' Co-operative, they cleared the litter, painted homes and lamp-posts and planted shrubs around the communal grassland. This initiative persuaded Oldham Council (the housing authority) to reverse its plans to demolish this part of the Sholver estate.

Tim Edge, Groundwork's Beal Valley Project Officer, heard about the work when the Groundwork Trust was approached by Sholver residents to help with a fencing project. He responded to the children's enthusiasm for more practical work and, with Martyn Atkinson, devised a programme of summer holiday activities. In the autumn of 1985, Tim organised projects around Sholver, walks in the countryside and trips further afield – for example, spending a day with a National Park ranger. The children were enthusiastic about these new experiences and enjoyed travelling in the minibus; they wanted to be 'rangers' like Tim, so they formed themselves into the Sholver Rangers.

By the middle of 1986, the Rangers had grown to a membership of 225 young people aged from 6 to 16. Up to 60 of them meet weekly in groups and they have developed a programme of activities which are organised mainly by Martyn and Tim with a team of 11 adult voluntary helpers – all residents on the estate, both employed and unemployed, male and female. 'We aim', says Martyn, 'not only to improve the local environment, but to give the kids some chance of developing confidence and self discipline to replace the boredom and destruction all around.'

The Rangers engage in a wide variety of activities, including after-school patrols on which they gather litter, protect nearby farmland from marauding dogs, note the stiles and fences that need repair, check that old people on the estate are safe and look out for vandals. A major project was born at one of the weekly meetings when Tim showed the Rangers a copy of the British Trust for Conservation Volunteers' Do-it-Yourself Conservation pack. They decided to develop their own Fullwood Nature Reserve – an area of nine hectares of scrub on the edge of the estate.

Here the Rangers have already cleared the rubbish, planted trees and are creating a range of wildlife habitats and building a bird hide. The plans, drawn up by the Groundwork Trust incorporating the Rangers' ideas, include a pond, paths and benches and an ambitious programme of new recreation areas on an adjoining site. Bulbs have been set in the autumn seasons as part of a wider Groundwork Campaign. And so far 1,800 trees have been planted. (Interestingly, an earlier attempt at tree planting on this site, by the local council without community involvement, had failed.)

Funding and management

There were three significant subsequent developments, in the spring of 1986:

- The council allowed the Rangers to use a nearby house on the estate as their base, and gave permission for work to be carried out on the Fullwood site. The Rangers pay a 'peppercorn' rent of 10p a year for both land and building.

- Following an application by Martyn Atkinson to the Royal Jubilee Trusts, £1,000 was granted and used to buy a minibus.

- A committee of management was established to administer the funds. It meets monthly and comprises: the Housing Department's Community Liaison Officer for Sholver, the Area Housing Manager, representatives from the Social Services Department, the local vicar, a local police officer, a schoolteacher, parents, two nominated Rangers, Tim Edge, Martyn Atkinson and other Ranger helpers.

In addition to the Jubilee Trusts' grant of £1,000, a Groundwork Trust Award of £200 bought a basic set of tools. In July 1986, Oldham Borough Council Housing Committee granted £1,500 to pay revenue costs in equipping and running the base over its first year. Among other items still needed are office furniture, a photocopier, computer and microscope, photographic and soil sampling materials. The Groundwork Trust continues to help in applying for funds on behalf of the Rangers. But capital and revenue funding is assured only for the current financial year. Insurance is provided under a local authority scheme and the Rangers are also covered by the Groundwork Trust's insurance for environmental work. One local company gave a set of yellow oilskins for the Rangers and items have been donated to equip the base.

Local benefits

All the Rangers are local young people, boys and girls. Their employment prospects are very poor, but there have been some successes. Martyn Atkinson tries to help them to get work in organisations like the National Park Authorities and the Forestry Commission but they need extra training to improve their chances. Two boys were placed on an agricultural Youth Training Scheme with a local farmer, and one plans to proceed to a polytechnic to take public examinations.

Life is not easy for young people on the estate. Their adult helpers try to deal with many problems – including truancy, crises at home and troubles with the police – by providing advice and practical support. There are now so many Rangers that Tim Edge and Martyn Atkinson are discussing ways of getting paid helpers – with seconded teachers or by employing trained youth workers, perhaps grant-aided through a Playboard scheme. Martyn Atkinson has enrolled on a management course at a local college and wants to train as a youth leader.

The results of the initiative are already impressive. With the Ranger patrols and a new security system, vandalism has declined on the estate: one estimate suggests that the council can save at least £30,000 on house repairs in three months. There is evidence that attitudes and habits are changing as a result of the Rangers' activity; residents meet more often and get on better. There are frequent celebrations in the nature reserve – bonfires and bar-b-cues, which involve adult residents.

In addition to the practical environmental work, which has given the Rangers a variety of skills, opportunities are constantly sought to foster their self-reliance. A group of 20 reached bronze medal standard in canoeing and are being trained in rock climbing as part of Greater Manchester Youth Action's 'Passport to Sport' programme. The Rangers thrive on activity and the learning which has been stimulated by their practical experience of the natural environment. Organisers are amazed at the enthusiasm – for learning wildlife names in Latin, for example. And the mobile library van is immediately picked clean of natural history books. Confidence is growing in many who have low self-esteem.

The role of the Groundwork Trust has been crucial – building upon grass-roots enthusiasm in a softly, softly way. Tim Edge works directly to the Executive Director of the Trust and reports to the Beal Valley Project Steering Committee. His involvement with the Sholver Rangers is purposely low key, helping where the Trust can – to mediate with council departments, accelerate decision-making where possible, suggest ideas, assist on applications for funding and give technical advice on publicity and practical environmental work. His is the role of 'enabler' and intermediary – encouraging (and sometimes curbing) enthusiasm but not destroying the Rangers' essential independence and spontaneity. 'It is vital', he says, 'that the Rangers organise themselves'. The Trust, meanwhile, is using the experience gained at Sholver on other run-down housing estates in its area, aiming to create neighbourhoods where people have some sense of belonging.

Community Support Anti-Waste Scheme

7 CSAWS' Recycling Team collect newspapers in Cardiff.

This community-based recycling scheme in Cardiff enables its membership of some 250 voluntary organisations to raise funds by collecting waste materials. The scheme has responded to other opportunities for waste-saving in the city by making household collections of paper and textiles, and renovating donated furniture which is sold cheaply to those in need. CSAWS began and still relies upon substantial volunteer effort, although it now employs 178 people.

Ten years ago, members of a youth club in Adamsdown, an inner city neighbourhood of Cardiff, began collecting and distributing newspapers and wood to local residents for their fires. But they soon amassed more than was needed and sold this to a paper merchant to raise funds. Local voluntary groups joined in, collecting paper and selling it through the youth club, beginning an assured supply for the merchant. In the club's sewing workshop, denim offcuts from a local factory were pieced into bags and skirts and sold on a market stall; the income was used to pay for club outings and camping trips.

In 1978, two MSC workers were recruited to run the recycling scheme, using two vehicles to collect cardboard from shops in the city centre, and waste paper from an increasing number of voluntary groups, each of whom gathered it from a different area of the city. One year later, 30 local groups were involved, including scouts, sports clubs, churches and schools. Meanwhile the recycling activities (including for a while, the sewing workshop) separated from the youth club to become first the Adamsdown Recycling Project, then CSAWS – Community Support Anti-Waste Scheme – and began a second MSC year under the Community Programme. There were 22 places – including a co-ordinator, liaison officer, and three supervisors.

With good publicity, 150 groups were soon collecting 20 tonnes of waste paper and textiles each week. CSAWS became the central collecting agency, storing the waste and negotiating a good price for it – even during the subsequent slump in waste paper prices – and returning most of the income back to the groups or to their chosen charities.

In 1979, to introduce some staff continuity and diversify its activities, CSAWS was formally constituted as a non-profit Friendly Society which applied for and was awarded a Urban Aid grant of £11,000 a year from Cardiff City Council for five years. Mike Croxford, a former hotel manager (who was liaison officer on the MSC scheme) became co-ordinator, and Bernard Shaw (previously a local disc jockey) became liaison officer.

While working with a local housing association and the citizens advice bureau to help pensioners move into smaller homes, CSAWS saw an opportunity to pass on surplus furniture to those who could make use of it. A shop was opened, first in Adamsdown, then in Ely, which sold the furniture cheaply to those in need – pensioners, unemployed people, single parents and others.

From 1979–86, CSAWS was run with these two full-time workers and six volunteers (drawn from a pool of 50–60) who collected, delivered and weighed the waste, and were paid £1 per day for meals and transport. Most were unemployed, and many were associated with the member groups. A good deal of time was spent in counselling volunteers and helping them to find paid work, lobbying on their behalf and talking to potential employers. Only lately have Mike Croxford and Bernard Shaw spent more time on project development and promotion. The current MSC scheme, begun in 1987, replaces the core of direct volunteers but these are still involved in other ways, especially promotion. Some give specialist help – with accountancy for example. Some former volunteers are now MSC workers.

The vision and commitment of the initial full-time workers and their co-ordination of volunteers, have been major elements in the expansion and diversification of CSAWS, in getting co-operation from local firms, and in sustaining the support of so many local groups. Overall, more than 18,000 volunteers are involved. Both the original workers are busy members of the local community, effective and enthusiastic about public relations – planning media stories, enlisting individual support, and participating in community events. When CSAWS won a Prince of Wales award for environment and community achievement, the visit of the Prince was an occasion for local celebration.

In 1984 CSAWS began sorting and grading office papers collected from commercial and statutory organisations on behalf of voluntary groups. Local companies like British Telecom and British Gas, and the University of Wales, were offered a confidential service for computer paper and letterheads (with locked skips, direct transport to merchants and shredding). Collection deals are now often arranged with particular firms through charitable members of CSAWS and these have released new sources of waste for recycling.

In December 1984, CSAWS moved into new premises in Splott, an inner city district of Cardiff, leased from Cardiff City Council at a peppercorn rent. An old council depot, this was refurbished by a Manpower Services Commission team and with monies made from recycling. Environmental improvements on the site (including planting and benches much used by local old people) were funded by the Prince of Wales' Committee and from Cardiff City's Inner Areas Improvement budget.

These new premises have become the base for a larger project including household waste collections and the repair of furniture and electrical goods. CSAWS' objectives are now economic, social and environmental:

- to help voluntary organisations raise funds through their participation in recycling

- to promote viable methods of collecting recyclable waste, providing a service which gives material and cost savings to society

- to create useful and satisfying jobs and training

- to promote local environmental improvement

With a core team of three, a further 175–person MSC Community Programme scheme began in 1987 which includes two elements: renovation and recycling.

Resource project
CSAWS collects unwanted furniture, identified by charitable groups, from homes in South Glamorgan. This is renovated in the carpentry workshops, providing training and jobs. More than 2,500 items have so far been refurbished. Income from the sale of the furniture (less the materials cost of renovation) is returned to the charity designated by the original owner of the furniture, providing

an incentive for further donations. Reject office furniture is also repaired for local groups.

The plan is to provide jobs and training for an increasing number of Cardiff's physically disabled people for whom the workshops have been especially designed (with an Urban Aid grant of £120,000). For John Midgeley, with 16 years on and off the dole suffering from haemophilia, the work offers a new lease of life, and the prospect of retraining in electrical repair. He looks forward to setting up his own business – a way of staying employed while coping with his disability. 'It is good', he says, 'to work on a scheme which helps me and does something for the community'.

Recycling project
CSAWS has begun the first monthly house-to-house collections of recyclable materials (paper, magazines, textiles and sump oil) in Wales, covering some 163,000 homes throughout the city. These collections fund part of CSAWS running costs, allowing more of the overall income from recycling to be returned to its member groups. Waste paper (120 tonnes each month) and textiles are sorted and stored in skips at the disused city abattoir, licensed from the City Council.

Management
CSAWS – now seeking charitable status – is guided by a management committee of 12 including two from the core team, officers and councillors from Cardiff City and South Glamorgan Councils, representatives of member groups, the Prince of Wales' Committee and a solicitor.

Staff training tries to promote an interest in recycling and the development of useful skills. Those working on the house collections are encouraged to talk to residents about recycling; staff outings are arranged to paper merchants and other recycling centres. Those working on furniture renovation can take a carpentry qualification at a local college and other courses are offered to all – on first aid, for example. Help is given with job searching towards the end of the MSC year.

CSAWS' success is built upon partnership – with voluntary organisations, business and the public sector. Local firms have helped in a number of ways: providing waste materials, sponsoring vehicles, a TV and video for training, and advising on legal matters and CSAWS' business plan. The latest development is the opening of a city-wide bottle bank network, funded initially by a major reclamation merchant, with the income going eventually to local groups who will manage the sites.

Cardiff City Council (the statutory waste collection and disposal authority) has designated CSAWS as its agent for recycling and refers residents there if they want to dispose of usable waste. The City Council leases the Splott base at a peppercorn rent, supplies two vehicles, contributed 25 per cent of the Urban Aid grant, and provides co-opted members of CSAWS management committee. And the scheme now has funding to work on a major recycling centre for Cardiff. This will offer residents and industry opportunities to reclaim a whole range of wastes at an accessible, landscaped site – open every day – where established and new recycling businesses can grow.

Hackney Grove Garden

8 Celebrations in Hackney Grove Garden.

Five years ago this secluded, sunken space was all that remained of a burnt-out toy factory. Hackney Council, owners of the half-acre derelict site, whose Housing Department overlooked it, proposed a car park. But local people – both residents and those who worked in premises fronting on to the Grove – had other ideas. They suggested a garden, with special facilities for the elderly and disabled, which could be used by many local groups.

In the autumn of 1981, Free Form, a Community Arts Trust in Hackney with experience of enabling local people to improve their surroundings, was asked to prepare a feasibility study, give technical assistance and cost out the plans. A successful application was made (through Hackney Borough Council) for Inner City Partnership funds of £72,000 over three years to build the garden. A subsequent allocation of £1,000 was made in 1985 to complete the masonry work and a fountain in one corner.

During the spring of 1982, Free Form brought together a variety of local organisations and individuals to form the Hackney Grove Garden Group and together with two landscape architects, who later implemented the scheme, they worked on the designs. These early discussions with potential users helped to identify just what was needed. A Dr Barnado's nursery, housed nearby, had no open space for play. 'Off Centre' – a young people's drop-in counselling centre directly opposite the site – wanted a place for outdoor activities and volunteered to form a team to help with gardening. Local groups involved in caring for the elderly and disabled wanted opportunities for them to garden. And in this part of Hackney, with the Housing Department and Town Hall nearby, it was clear that casual use by passers-by and space for lunchtime picnickers had to be planned for. During this time negotiations also took place with the Greater London Council to link the garden to a cycleway running through Hackney Grove.

How it works
The overall concept is based upon a gently sloping, curving path (suitable for wheelchairs and bicycles), which runs through the site, finishing at a small level area which can be used for performance. The garden is terraced down from the road to this space, creating a sheltered amphitheatre with many seating areas set amongst boulders and vegetation. In terms of design, the garden works on two levels: from outside (where many 'users' in neighbouring offices experience it) and inside.

Outside, from the Grove, the garden appears as an oasis of life and colour beneath the drab walls which enclose it on three sides. In spite of its shaded aspect the image is exotic: careful planting of evergreen trees and shrubs gives some winter cover as well as a variety of colour changes throughout the growing season. Two features dominate the garden from outside – a mural with trellis work on one wall and the stylish blue and green railings which front onto the Grove on either side of the garden's entrance gate. The railings were designed by Free Form and commissioned from an ironsmith. They are one of a number of innovative design ideas pioneered in this garden, which have since been used in other community projects on which Free Form has worked. To make the most of the whole space – the garden site and its surroundings – the adjacent Hackney Housing Department was persuaded to refurbish its own car park as part of construction work on the garden. The blue and green railings link both developments and the whole approach to the Grove is now more interesting – and inviting.

Inside the garden, attention is directed away from the ugly surrounding buildings and on to a rich and amusing variety of detailed features which have been built into the walls and paths. Much has been salvaged from other building sites: a gravestone, masonry faces and other figures. Retaining walls incorporate interesting and unusual brickwork, waterfalls and a good deal of children's art including brightly coloured mosaics and clay models. Wooden archways, stone and wooden window frames and doors all enhance the visual diversity and provide opportunities for imaginative and adventurous play.

The vegetation is unusual for a small city garden, with much use of eucalyptus, rhododendron and bamboo. But this has stood up well to heavy wear and, by suppressing weed growth, is easy to maintain. With an award from the Shell Better Britain Campaign, a shallow pond and small natural area is being created.

The garden was substantially complete in two years, at a final cost of £73,000. It is in use daily by passers by and has been visited regularly by pre-schoolers from a nearby nursery, primary school children, disabled gardeners from a hostel for the handicapped and psychiatric patients from Hackney hospital who helped with its construction.

Management

At least three times a year there are special garden 'workdays' organised by the Hackney Grove Garden Group who apply each year to Hackney Borough Council for a contribution to garden maintenance and the organisation and publication of celebrations: £2,000 was allocated last year. Other events – drama and concerts – and a host of more informal activities take place in the performance space. There is little vandalism and litter is cleared frequently by volunteers. Confetti testifies to the garden's increasing use for wedding photographs in a neighbourhood where there are no other green open spaces.

From inception to the present, local people have played a major part in the garden. They worked with Free Form on its design and with the contractors on its creation. There have been frequent celebrations, both during and after the garden was made. Now volunteers maintain it and manage its use.

Jane Sugarman, chair of the Hackney Grove Garden Group, thinks its role is still a crucial one in the life of the garden: 'We try to organise the maintenance and find new ways of involving local people.' Future plans include further planting along a blank wall, sunflower-growing competitions and greater efforts to get nearby secondary schools to play a part in maintenance and use the garden for study. As one of a green necklace of community gardens around London, Hackney Grove is an active member of the North London Community Gardens Association, hosting regular meetings with other members to exchange ideas, experience and celebrations.

5 More Jobs, New Enterprise

Most of the initiatives studied have at some time sponsored MSC job creation programmes, especially the Community Programme (CP), to augment the small number of staff funded in other ways. For some, especially the local energy and recycling projects, CP staff continue to make up the bulk of their personnel. And these are often large schemes: Avon FOE's compendium of resourceful schemes has 200 CP places (page 21), Brass Tacks employs 123 (page 70). Neighbourhood Energy Action calculates that some 8,000 people are presently employed on 430 local energy schemes.

It is clear that local environmental action sponsored by voluntary organisations can provide highly satisfying work. Most of the paid staff interviewed, including unskilled workers with no previous commitment to environmental action, placed some value not only on the skills they were acquiring but the contribution their work was making towards social and environmental improvement. The most satisfying jobs seem to be those that combine all of these qualities, produce an obvious local gain and allow considerable social contact – both within a working team, and with the public. Some work is considered intrinsically boring – especially collecting household wastes – but it has been possible for schemes to improve job satisfaction here, by diversifying tasks, increasing public contact and encouraging interest in the subject through trips and talks in the training programme. As other studies have shown, job satisfaction, particularly among less skilled MSC participants, is closely related to the quality of supervision and training provided.

A wide range of skills can be associated with environmental projects including: manual work, trade and craft skills (in electrical repair and furniture restoration, for example), professional training (especially in horticulture and landscape management), administration and accountancy. Some of the projects, notably the recycling workshops, place great emphasis on the training offered, and see themselves mainly as training initiatives.

A number of the environmental initiatives studied have a good record of employing those from disadvantaged groups who often find it harder than usual to get employment – disabled people, ethnic minorities, those with a recent history of mental ill-health and women. Indeed for some schemes, it is a declared objective to attract these groups, and efforts are directed towards specialist advertising (for example in the ethnic press) and specialist training – where this has been possible within highly restricted budgets.

It is clear that some of the schemes have provided a particularly supportive and caring environment for disadvantaged people to be rehabilitated, increasing their confidence, self-esteem and sometimes their prospects of finding permanent jobs. Andrew McArthur notes: 'It is difficult to put a price on the boost to morale and quality of life which might result, but it remains an important contribution in terms of community development'.[35]

Environmental projects vary in their ability to place CP employees in subsequent work or training, but of those that keep detailed records, most appear to do better than the average for all CP schemes, and some do much better (an MSC national survey showed that an average of 25 per cent of those leaving CP schemes go on to more permanent jobs, a third go on to jobs or further training). The amount of help given with job searching varies; most would like to spend more time and effort than they do on this, preparing their MSC workers for interviews, advertising their skills, and making links with potential local employers.

PROBLEMS WITH THE COMMUNITY PROGRAMME

All groups experienced the now familiar problems of Community Programme funding, some of which hit environmental projects especially hard. The main limitations, both for action and the personal development of CP workers, may be summarised as follows:

• Schemes have to reapply annually to MSC for renewal, which gives an atmosphere of continual uncertainty and takes up valuable time in administration and away from action. This uncertainty can be unnecessarily costly, as when one project was required repeatedly to hire a training film rather than buy it. Projects are not encouraged to behave like businesses and plan ahead.

• The maximum 52 week contract for participants has meant a constantly changing workforce, with participants low in morale at the start of a contract and distracted by uncertainty and job searching at the end. The incentive of promotion cannot be used as a management tool (nor does the MSC offer any other recognition of good work, although projects have introduced their own incentives).

• The £67 per week average wage level has meant that for realistic wage rates to be offered, most participants have to be part-time, effectively halving a 52 week contract, reducing opportunities for training, and often a participant's commitment and morale. This is considered to be too short a period for effective skills training in many of the environmental initiatives studied – especially greening schemes, where experience of several growing seasons is required, and waste renovation projects where the development of subsequently usable skills takes at least a full year of work and training. And part-time working means that too little time is available to participants for training in personal and life skills – including help, for example, with literacy, with CV and interview preparation for subsequent jobs, with becoming self-employed and starting a business.

• Because the CP is fundamentally a work experience programme, the training that can be offered within the rules is limited in other ways; many unskilled part-time participants complained that training was not long enough or sufficiently thorough to fit them for subsequent employment. Project staff invariably wanted more flexibility, cash and full-time staff to improve training. Some wanted more resources to prepare individual portfolios for their participants to help them in job searching and to make links with local employers.

• Most schemes have experienced difficulties in attracting good quality supervisors and sometimes retaining them beyond a year – vital if continuity is to be maintained. Nor are there resources to train supervisors and other senior staff in the personnel management skills needed – working with ethnic minorities, for example.

• The small number of supervisory staff has meant inadequate management (both for participants and to accommodate any volunteers) and some poor quality work.

• Management time is often severely stretched in constantly organising and training new staff, leaving none for forward planning, developing new initiatives and fund raising. Sometimes, the quality of project work could not be sustained or improved.

• Schemes risk a clawback of any trading surplus and are discouraged from managing an enterprise in ways which could increase trading returns and the degree of self-funding.

• London schemes criticise the lack of London weighting attached to MSC wage rates in a city where the cost of living is higher than elsewhere.

Projects that now have MSC Managing Agency status (like Avon FOE and Keeping Newcastle Warm) have overcome some of these problems, for this allows extra funds to be spent on administrative and research support and staff training and gives more security that a scheme will continue to operate beyond a year, encouraging managers to plan ahead. Some of the problems have also been addressed in recent changes of MSC CP policy (especially in connection with the UK 2000 programme). The supervisor:participant ratio has improved and it is possible for project agents and sponsors to negotiate two-year contracts for some managers and supervisors.

Other policy changes have been recommended for environmental projects: that managers and supervisors should be appointed for up to five years to provide continuity; that projects should be able to appoint volunteer co-ordinators, and apply for development funds and the resources to improve training. But while the MSC has recognised the need for more training and encourages it, no extra funding has been available.

Following a number of analyses of the Community Programme,[36] the MSC is now committed to improving its quality and management, specifically to:

- improving individual chances for permanent jobs or training, including those at a disadvantage in the labour market (for example, disabled people and ethnic minorities)

- maximising community benefits – to have a lasting impact and assist area regeneration (so priority will go to inner city areas covered by City Action Teams and Task Forces)

- improving the mobilisation of public and private sector funds

- augmenting other public policies

Enterprise is also to be fostered. In a number of pilot areas (now being extended) CP participants can elect to set up 'Enterprise Projects' in the last three months of their CP year, trading commercially and testing out business ideas developed earlier. Extra funds are available for training and enterprise advice, and any profits are held over to support the new venture. This scheme, it is hoped, will encourage entrepreneurs and ease the transition to self-employment.

Other recent and proposed CP changes are more problematic. Participants now have to be continuously unemployed for a year to qualify and priority is given to those aged between 25 and 50 (most participants on environmental schemes are presently under 25). Payment at the 'rate for the job' is threatened by government plans to link CP to benefit entitlement plus a premium, later in 1988 (combining CP with the Job Training Scheme). One result could be reduced local authority and union support for environmental CP schemes. And these projects, of community benefit, seem likely to be allocated fewer places and face increased difficulty in attracting highly motivated participants.[37] There is as yet no assurance of more resources for improved training.

Problems are arising as the CP nears its target of 240,000 nationally and there is increasing competition for places. Some local energy schemes, for example, are facing difficulties in recruiting suitable staff. Other initiatives may find it difficult to start up, or to expand, especially where they do not qualify under the MSC's defined National Initiatives, which include environmental improvement (UK 2000), and energy efficiency.

New businesses

A number of the initiatives studied have been successful in spawning independent environmental enterprises. Although the scale is small, these businesses sustain permanent jobs – each around six or less. They are organised in a variety of ways, often as co-operatives or informal partnerships of the self-employed.

They show that it is possible for previously unemployed people to use a period of environmental volunteering, or (more usually) a Community Programme year to try out ideas and working relationships and acquire the confidence, skills and market knowledge to set up an enterprise. Of those studied, most had not been in business before and had not considered themselves as entrepreneurs. Most took advantage of the MSC Enterprise Allowance Scheme and all are still trading after that year (perhaps surprising in view of the high failure rate for small businesses generally).

But their future is uncertain. Some of the businesses are very fragile: waste (and especially newspaper) collection schemes are particularly vulnerable to fluctuating raw material prices. Turnovers are small, long hours are worked, often for low wage rates (less or no better than the £3 per hour common on CP schemes). But optimism and commitment are high. It is clear that the challenge of 'going it alone' increases job satisfaction. And concern for the welfare of workers is strong, even where the enterprise is not organised as a co-operative. The work is varied, the management democratic.

Some of these new enterprises combine many of the objectives of the parent scheme and retain close links with that scheme and other satellites, in a synergistic relationship of mutual aid (see, for example, those of Avon FOE on page 18 and the UCAT enterprises, page 39). These parent initiatives correspond to what McArthur has called 'micro development agencies'.[38]

In the new businesses, there is often a firm commitment to environmental and social values as well as a desire to be profitable. And there is an emphasis upon providing high quality goods and services. In this way, the enterprises often have a 'community business' flavour – of allegiance to the needs of the locality even if their management does not include community representatives (see, for example, the Camden Garden Centre, page 75, Paperback, page 80). It is doubtful whether any of the enterprises could have started up without help on premises: most have managed to find low rent/ low rate space from their parent scheme or from some other supporting agency, usually in the public sector. But few initiatives have been as adventurous as the furniture renovation workshops – Camden Recycling Ltd – in persuading the council to fund an adjacent set of starter business units to let at low rents to those coming off their CP year.

The extent to which these small enterprises create new work or simply displace existing jobs is hard to gauge. There is some evidence that entirely new markets have been created by new 'green' goods and services – as with Blackwall Products' composting 'tumbler', Avon FOE's Energy Services and perhaps the Camden Garden Centre. Certainly, infant markets have been extended in size – as with Paperback's and Arboreta's promotion of recycled paper products, or Landlife's sales of wild flower seeds – though all at an unknown cost to sales of other, less environmentally-friendly goods. And although some initiatives have spawned fairly conventional new businesses (upholstery, carpentry and electrical repair in the case of Camden Recycling Ltd), it is possible that their work on renovating formerly wasted goods has enlarged the overall market for these services.

Problems of 'microfirms'

A study of *Local Enterprise and the Unemployed* sponsored by the Gulbenkian Foundation developed the concept of the 'microfirm':

... the type of enterprise that might be established by an unemployed person, or someone recently made redundant. It could be a very small conventional limited company, or a group of individuals working together, or a sole trader ... [The definition concerns] community enterprises, worker co-operatives, neighbourhood co-operatives and community trading. The microfirm typically has limited capital and serves a local market.[39]

The study found that existing small firms support policies were not sensitive to the needs of these very small businesses or the needs of 'untried entrepreneurs' on the Enterprise Allowance Scheme.

Like other 'micro firms', the 'green' enterprises studied here have all found difficulties in starting up – both in persuading finance houses to take them seriously and back them, and also in getting access to business advice (especially on marketing and pricing) which is detailed enough to be helpful for their particular scheme. Their unconventional ideas for enterprise and their attitudes (for example towards the environment, or the need for high quality) have sometimes brought ridicule from those approached for support. The Small Firms Service and local Enterprise Agencies have too little experience of less conventional businesses to offer this specialist advice. The services of the Greater London Enterprise Board, which helped Blackwall Products and Paperback to start up (and in the case of Blackwall, to test out an innovative idea) seem to be exceptions here.

Future directions

The suggestion from a number of those interviewed from environmental CP schemes was that, given more flexibility, the ability to advertise and trade more openly to assess what markets exist locally, and the capacity to train potential entrepreneurs better, then more self-funding 'green' enterprises could be nurtured. It was felt that this flexibility could be accommodated within MSC policy (which precludes CP schemes from competing with the private sector), for the enterprises are likely to open up new niches in the local market rather than compete with existing traders. The CP 'Enterprise Projects' experiment could help here if it is extended beyond the present pilot areas.

The markets for these new enterprises are sometimes highly local, and often no more than borough or district-wide. And the market conditions would seem to be widely replicable, suggesting that the potential is there for many more to start up, given support. Not all the enterprises are dealing at the margins, in goods and services of intrinsically low profitability. And even where they are, there may be ways of combining the more- and less-profitable operations in one viable enterprise. Richard Moulson and John Newson conclude:

Many recycling activities, if considered as single, separate businesses seem unable to cover both wage costs and all overheads, which is why the sector is commercially undeveloped. However, there is a strong case for thinking that a cluster of such businesses (including repair and new products from waste) could exist by cross-subsidising and sharing overheads such as personnel, premises, publicity, collections and transport . . . A single Recycling Centre would have many advantages.[40]

Interestingly, the lack of effective marketing was blamed for the declining fortunes of Windcheaters in Bristol (page 41) and Warmth, an energy co-operative in Tower Hamlets (page 100) and the vulnerability of a number of the other new businesses. For some, contracts from local authorities and other public bodies have been vital in sustaining their viability in the early stages, while new markets could be explored. Warmth, the Lewisham Energy Centre (now employing 10) and Edinburgh Draughtproofing Ltd have all depended on this early support.[41] It it likely that imaginative local authority contracting (not only on insulation and energy advice, but on paper supplies, furniture repair and other recycled goods, and city greening) could help more environmental enterprises to flourish.

Hackney Brass Tacks

9 Selling renovated furniture at the Brass Tacks shop in Hackney.

Housed in a converted sweatshop, near Dalston Junction, the Brass Tacks Workshops renovate unwanted furniture and electrical goods and sell them cheaply to low income families. The scheme was established in 1979 by the Mutual Aid Centre, a charitable foundation which promotes small-scale practical experiments in co-operation and self-help, especially those which create jobs.

In 1980, there were just 30 on the Brass Tacks staff; now, as a Community Programme initiative, it provides work and training for 123 of Hackney's long-term unemployed. The primary aim is work experience. But the managers see individual training and personal development as equal objectives and refer to staff as 'trainees' rather than 'participants'. There are also community and, indirectly, environmental benefits. The renovated household goods are available to low-income families. And Brass Tacks is seen as a local response to global problems of resource waste.

Some difficulty is acknowledged in combining these social, economic and environmental goals, especially as the scheme's funders (MSC and Hackney Council) and sponsor (Mutual Aid Centre) have different priorities. One example of practical conflict is in the running of the shop: managing this to increase revenue could improve business training and generate more income. But there may then be fewer goods available cheaply; increasing productivity could conflict with training; financial surpluses would be clawed back by the MSC.

Brass Tacks houses a shop and seven workshops, with an average of eight trainees and one supervisor in each. All departments are considered as training areas, including the shop, finance office, the small building maintenance group, and (until recently) a call-out team that helped local people with minor house repairs. The departments are:

- *Upholstery*: a major problem here, as in the restoration workshop, is the lack of good quality furniture to repair which would provide a better training opportunity, increases motivation and sells for more.

- *Sewing*: trainees learn to design and make goods from scrap cloth. Early on in the course, they produce items for sale, and can see the effect of their choice of materials and workmanship on sales.

- *Furniture restoration*: the supervisor aims to increase the number of quality items for repair by buying some furniture from auctions.

- *Woodworking*: trainees make new furniture from items that are impossible to restore and from waste wood from a local firm.

- *Polishing and finishing*: trainees complete renovations begun in the woodworking and restoration workshops.

- *Electrical*: here too it is sometimes difficult to get white goods adequate for repair.

- *Electronics workshop*: all staff come with two years of training.

- *Shop*: this sells mainly to those on supplementary benefit, referred from the DHSS and other welfare agencies.

- *Maintenance team*: originally converted and continues to maintain the premises.

Until recently, there was a call-out team of one supervisor and two part-time trainees who attended to minor repairs in the borough when referred to the homes of elderly and disabled people, and low-income families, by the DHSS and other welfare agencies. The team incidentally provided companionship and advice on other repairs needed, referring cases to the relevant local authority department.

Management and funding
Now 123 people work at Brass Tacks, including 112 CP participants (of which 106 are part-time). There are 11 full-time supervisors and managers. Most are appointed from the job centre and ethnic mino-

rities, especially West Indians, are well represented. Where possible, those who find it harder than most to get work are employed: offenders, disabled people, educationally deprived, and those who have been recently ill or suffered some other difficult period in their lives. Many have never worked. Employees are mainly unskilled, except in the electronics workshop. Some are illiterate and are guided to literacy classes. When selecting its staff, Brass Tacks tries to match their interests and any skills they have to the needs of specific workshops. And there is also an attempt to encourage equal opportunities – women in woodworking, men in sewing crafts.

Morale is low when the new trainees arrive. All the supervisors interviewed spoke of their confidence increasing through the work year. The caring, friendly and sociable environment, with supervisors paying much attention to individual needs, provides a year of rehabilitation and improving self-esteem: 'we are recycling people' says the finance manager. For Harry Levison, upholstery supervisor, seeing this transformation makes the job worthwhile and compensates for the low rates of pay. Now close to retirement, he has and enjoys a pastoral role. Roy Lansiquot, an assembly line worker before he was unemployed, came first as a trainee and is now wood working supervisor. He likes the teaching and is convinced 'there is something good here for people who have been out of work for long periods'.

The trainees' practical experience in the workshops is supported by tuition one day each week at local education centres where one third of them study for City and Guilds qualifications in upholstery, polishing or cabinet making, or take academic or commercial subjects. Fees and fares are paid. Hackney College arranges short courses to update late-joining staff.

A DHSS basic tools allowance encourages some trainees to continue practising on their days off. And there are other incentives to do well: trainees get a reference and a certificate, and keep portfolios of photographs of their work (although this requires extra supervision time which is difficult to find).

All receive life and social skills training throughout the year, including an induction period in which there is some discussion of recycling issues. Advice is available on benefits and personal matters from a welfare surgery and in the last quarter, trainees are counselled on job searching, with practice on interview techniques, CVs, and letter writing. The aim is to provide more help here, for example, by making links with local employers.

A majority of Brass Tacks employees go on to permanent employment or more training: in 1987, 70 per cent found full-time jobs, 3 per cent returned to full-time education. Some past trainees have set up new businesses, including (in 1985) one self-employed upholsterer and an upholstery co-operative of two: 'Second Time Around' – both formerly housed in the Brass Tacks building.

The continual staff turnover can be disruptive for the scheme; time-keeping is poor when trainees start and when they are job searching near the end of their work year, but there is little absentee-ism. Part-time employment reduces motivation, discourages good timekeeping and disrupts training; most participants want to work full-time. But it is usually impossible to promote participants or supervisors and motivate them in this way. Good supervisors are crucial and often difficult to replace (on wage rates of £8,500). They need practical skills, maturity to cope with the pastoral care, and the ability to generate enthusiasm, yet face the annual uncertainty of their job being renewed.

A management team of 11 (including Project Manager, Deputy, Finance Manager and 8 supervisors) is guided by the Brass Tacks board of six directors. A Works Council of elected staff members and management representatives meets monthly. Most administration (for this and a number of other recycling schemes) is now handled by the Mutual Aid Centre MSC Managing Agency.

Brass Tacks' annual budget is £1/2 million. The MSC pay the labour costs of £360,000 and so substantial is this sum that the prospect of Brass Tacks 'unhooking' from MSC is slim. Extra funding of £35,000 comes from Hackney Borough Council, under the Urban Programme. This covers running costs, including heating and lighting, tools and materials, but continual cuts have made the future uncertain.

All the household goods are donated for renovation, and collec-tion is free. The shop contributes £18,000 per year (a third of the revenue funding) which is also spent on tools and materials. Each item costs some £20 to be renovated through the workshops and every stage is costed in detail. The aim is to cut workshop costs further and increase sales – with better marketing (more attractive arrangements in the shop and improved advertising), and with more attention to producing goods of the type that customers want to buy. But both cost-cutting and increased revenue are limited by the training and social objectives of the scheme; even goods that do not sell are nevertheless valuable for training.

Community Programme rules mean that Brass Tacks must not compete with private traders. But there would seem to be no direct competition here, for the service is unique: goods are donated and repaired for resale, adding value, providing work and skills training.

Brass Tacks rent the premises from Hackney Council and have, at various times, sublet space to a number of other initiatives, including Bootstrap Enterprises, printers, building co-operative (formerly staff of the call-out team), electrical repair business, upholstery co-operative, picture-framer, restaurant and the Brass Tacks Nursery. The upholstery co-operative 'Second Time Around' was set up by two former Brass Tacks trainees who learnt all their skills on the scheme and built up a business from commissioned work.

Camden Garden Centre

10 Training in horticultural and social skills is an important objective at Camden Garden Centre.

This experimental garden centre has transformed a triangle of wasteland and is designed to become a self-sustaining enterprise with social as well as commercial objectives – aiming to increase the employment and training opportunities for young people in a multi-racial community.

The garden was established in 1982 as the second venture of the Southern Task Educational Trust which is concerned, in a number of community enterprises, with job creation and training. The trust was initiated by Gurmukh Singh, a local businessman, and includes representatives of the Wellcome Foundation and other local people.

The site of just less than one acre, originally designated for public housing, was leased from Camden Council for three years at a rent of £5,000 per year – below commercial rates. A start-up loan of £100,000 was secured from a local bank, guaranteed by the Wellcome Foundation which has its offices in the area. This followed a feasibility study by the London Business School (also paid for by Wellcome) which showed a likely market in the Camden Town/Kentish Town area and a potential turnover of £250,000 in the first year.

The gardens were constructed by the staff and first trainees, the covered area was architect-designed and built by contractors. The Tudor Trust gave £2,000 and garden suppliers helped in kind. Marks and Spencer gave some free advice on arranging the retailing area; the London Business School have given advice informally.

How it works

The centre is well stocked with garden and house plants, and related products, especially those suitable for urban environments – patios, backyards and window boxes. 'Our aim' said Richard Jackson, the centre's first manager, 'is to make gardening easier and more adventurous for people who live in towns'. Great plant variety has been packed into a small space, with much use of vertical structures – trellises and pergolas. There is a 35-space car park and the centre caters for disabled gardeners.

There is much emphasis upon the high quality of the products and services the centre offers. Staff are well informed and ready to advise. Early on, to build up the market, there was a plant hire service, personal, home-based garden advice and a 'plant doctor' for emergency help.

The garden centre began with seven full-time trainees (and now employs 10), a manager and deputy manager, a part-time administrator and part-time driver. Staff are drawn from the job centre and ethnic minorities are well represented. Training is a major objective of the scheme, and includes horticulture, advising customers and participating in management. There are briefings from nurserymen, trips to famous gardens, and all the trainees study one day each week for a City and Guilds qualification in horticulture. But the aim is also to provide them with the necessary management and social skills that may be useful later in running a business of their own.

Trainees work a probationary week and are selected for enthusiasm rather than knowledge or qualifications: few have any previous gardening experience. Each takes responsibility for a particular section of the garden, such as seeds, pot plants, hanging baskets.

The scheme seems to have been successful in improving individual confidence and self-esteem and preparing trainees for further work. All of the first seven trainees went on to full-time jobs (five in horticulture), one left to become assistant manager at another similar garden centre. Most of the subsequent trainees have also found paid work, in a variety of jobs; indeed there is now a problem with the high turnover of staff.

Much of the credit for building up the business quickly and developing the centre's reputation for a well-informed and enthusiastic staff must go to the first manager, Richard Jackson, a trained horticulturalist with a democratic style of management incorporating considerable sharing of decisions and delegation of responsibility. Camden Garden Centre Ltd is guided by a board of directors which includes two representatives from the original trust, and the Wellcome Foundation.

Financially, the centre must be judged a success, exceeding expectations in its first year of trading with a turnover of £320,000. In 1986/87 the turnover was £500,000. There is a profit-sharing scheme for staff; and some of the profits are returned to the trust to start up other ventures, which include a building and landscaping business – Camden Landscaping – and a garden centre in Brixton.

Blackwall Products Ltd

11 The revolutionary 'Tumbler' which turns vegetable waste into garden compost in 21 days.

In a doubly waste-saving operation, this co-operative turns discarded plastic barrels into composting units, which can convert kitchen and garden waste to compost in record time.

Grant Blakemore and Ian Taylor (a graduate engineer) both with interests in recycling and job creation, developed the idea of the 'Tumbler' in the workshops of the London Energy and Employment Network (LEEN) during 1984. Both had experience of manufacturing industry and of working with unemployed people and wanted to be practically involved in creating new jobs.

Encouraged by the former GLC's Recycling Unit, they sought and received backing from the Greater London Enterprise Board in September 1984. This included funding for a feasibility study, then, following submission of a business plan, a start-up loan of £70,000 (£45,000 from GLEB and £25,000 from the London Co-operative Enterprise Board – both to be repaid over five years). The company – Blackwall Products Ltd – was launched in 1985 to produce and market the 'Tumbler'.

Taylor and Blakemore acknowledge the importance of a combination of supports: early encouragement from the GLC and GLEB, the emphasis GLEB placed on careful business planning, the business advice that was offered, and the swiftly-arranged financial support. The London Borough of Greenwich provided invaluable assistance with low-cost premises.

The barrels (bought from importers of fruit juice, olives and other products) are washed, drilled and spray-painted and set on tubular aluminium frames (originally shaped in the Thames TechNet workshop) which allow the barrels to rotate. It is the tumbling motion which is innovative – allowing grass clippings and other vegetable waste to be aerated to produce compost in 21 days. A liquid fertiliser can also be prepared. The production and marketing emphasis is upon a high quality, well-finished product.

Blackwall's office and workshop premises were first rented at a favourable rate from the Thames TechNet (the SE London Technology and Employment Network – a GLEB funded training centre). Now, needing more space, the co-op has moved and rents buildings on a council trading estate. The London Borough of Greenwich helped with an 18 month rent grant and financial assistance towards the construction of an office.

The former GLC Recycling Unit promoted the enterprise in its early days by producing publicity leaflets and sharing its stand at the 1985 Ideal Home Exhibition with Blackwall Products. This allowed the 'Tumbler' to be displayed, led to the first orders and to an exhibit at the Chelsea Flower Show (and more orders). Most sales – some 1,000 each month – are by mail order response to advertisements and leaflets, distributed at first with the Recycling Unit's publicity. In 1986, the predicted market (25,000 per year) seemed large enough to justify much more advertising, and the appointment of a retailing agent – now Blackwall sells to a number of major home care retailers.

The co-operative provides full-time employment for five and part-time work for one. Four of the co-op's staff were unemployed before they joined. 'We are all', says Grant Blakemore, 'interested in environmental issues, and keen to promote recycling and organic gardening methods'. Job satisfaction is high and increased by rotating the mechanical tasks weekly. Composting is highly seasonal, so the co-op is developing other ideas to diversify its products. Some barrels are already sold as water butts, and other garden goods have been developed, including a tubular framed seed house, seed trays and polythene sheeting.

Paperback Ltd

12 Jan Kuiper – Paperback pioneer.

This co-operative in Hackney has pioneered new markets for recycled paper and paper products.

Motivated by an environmental concern about resource waste and pollution, and drawing on his experience of the Netherlands (where the use of recycled papers is much more common), Jan Kuiper established a small co-operative with two others in 1983. All had previously worked or campaigned with environmental organisations, but were unemployed before starting the co-operative.

The Greater London Enterprise Board (GLEB) provided business courses, advice on a business plan, and a loan of £12,000 at an interest rate of 5 per cent. This secured an overdraft of £3,000 from a local bank, and Hackney Council (through its Economic Development Unit) also paid a start-up capital grant and a two-year rent grant. The business began by selling a narrow range of recycled duplicating paper and stationery – having extensively researched the potential market in a feasibility study and through a market stall.

Paperback is now a paper merchant and wholesale supplier of a wide range of recycled papers and paper products to an increasing number of national environmental and voluntary organisations and local authorities. It sells specialist recycled papers to other paper merchants and supplies shops with packs of paper, envelopes and cards for retailing, but no longer sells its products by mail order. The turnover in 1985 was £82,000, in 1986, £120,000 and in 1987, £300,000.

In 1986 Paperback set up a consortium of recycled paper sellers (which includes Arboreta – see page 22) to buy papers in bulk from the mills and negotiate reduced prices. Jan Kuiper thinks this makes a vital link between producers and consumers, and is one way of increasing recycled paper production to meet an expanding and diversifying market. Good relations have been established with several paper mills: the consortium is able to communicate customers' needs. One mill has been persuaded to produce the first matt-coated recycled paper for printing – to a specification designed by Kuiper.

Paperback mails its catalogue widely, trying to persuade voluntary organisations (especially environmental ones) to adopt recycled office papers. Local authorities are beginning to change to recycled paper for copying and duplicating: Paperback supplies some of the paper needs of five London boroughs and hopes to increase the market here steadily rather than rapidly, so that the mills can build up their production.

The co-operative is aiming for more retail outlets but admits that marketing needs to be developed to reach the main stationery chains. The aim is to open up new niches in the paper market: printers and designers are the latest target. Kuiper tries to persuade them to exploit the special qualities of recycled papers, rather than treat them as poor substitutes for conventional materials. Raising general public awareness is a subsidiary objective of Paperback: publicity leaflets which accompany the catalogue describe the advantages of recycling, and stress the importance of using recycled products as well as saving and collecting paper waste.

Management and funding
Paperback provides full-time employment for four (in office and computer management, finance and personnel management, marketing, buying and selling) and part-time work for a driver. Early on the jobs were rotated, but the business has come to demand increasing specialisation. All staff attend periodic courses organised by the co-operative movement on, for example, financial management, marketing and social skills. Wages, having been very low in the first few years, are now some £160 a week for all members of the group. A small number of unemployed volunteers help in the office – learning accountancy and marketing skills.

The co-operative was launched with a low-interest loan of £12,000, and received a further loan of £5,000 from GLEB in 1986 to install a computer and new telephones. In 1987, Paperback was grant-aided under the government's 'Support for Design' scheme to commission a designer to produce a new corporate image for the company, including sample books, brochure and stationery. A five-year marketing plan is in preparation, as a precursor to raising long-term finance.

A major problem now is the lack of working capital to finance expansion: Paperback needs larger and more appropriate (ground floor) premises for the office and warehouse, and wants to develop new products and a promotional strategy. Finding no success with conventional sources of finance, Paperback has been forced to consider other innovative ways of raising the necessary capital for expansion: the company now plans to issue 'debenture stock' in March 1988. Industrial Common Ownership Finance (ICOF), GLEB and Hackney's Co-operative Development Agency have all helped with the development of the idea, marketing it and preparing a prospectus.

Finding mutually accountable methods of co-operative working is a perennial management issue. Jobs are now more clearly specified and sales and financial details are monitored monthly. Some conflict is acknowledged in trying to marry ideological objectives (about the environment and co-operative working) with the need for commercial success: collective decisions take longer. Even so, the co-operative structure is felt to be a marketing asset. Paperback sees itself as innovative both technically, managerially – and now financially.

6 Making It Happen

The scope for local environmental initiatives to be more effective in creating work depends in part upon how successfully they can tackle other problems that hinder progress. Some of these are common to many projects in the voluntary sector; others are a consequence of the relative youthfulness of much practical environmental work in the city – projects and organisations are at early stages in their life cycle.

Yet many problems can be seen as opportunities, and are being overcome in the best schemes, which provide valuable lessons for good practice. This chapter discusses in turn: access to land and buildings, funding, staffing, technical aid, training, evaluation of performance, management structure, community involvement and links with other agencies. Each section tries to suggest the immediate obstacles to be overcome and hints at longer-term opportunities.

ACCESS TO LAND AND BUILDINGS

Delays and other difficulties of cost and ownership here may limit a group's enthusiasm. The most successful schemes have managed to lease or license land and buildings cheaply, even if the use is only to be temporary. Opportunities to negotiate access need to be improved and a local authority's role here can be crucial: only a few already have a contact point where local groups can be helped to find vacant land to manage for community uses. The London Borough of Camden funds a small unit called 'Growth Unlimited' to do this over the whole borough. The unit responds to requests from voluntary organisations and community groups, stimulates action and co-ordinates activities, enabling groups to share information and experience.

Finding suitable premises is another major problem for projects: high rents and rates can absorb much of their running costs. Local authorities can often help to locate office and storage space, or provide these at low cost.

A number of case studies show the importance of local technical aid centres and other 'enabling' groups in acting as intermediaries between voluntary organisations and property owners (public and private) to facilitate access to land and buildings.

FUNDING

Environmental initiatives in the UK can draw on a variety of central government funding sources, including grant aid in England from the Department of Environment (under the Urban Programme, Urban Initiatives, Special Grants and Derelict Land Programmes).[42] The Countryside Commission and Nature Conservancy Council offer grants for work in the urban fringe and countryside, and the Manpower Services Commission (MSC) can pay labour and administrative costs for approved projects under a number of special employment schemes such as the Community Programme. In terms of central government funding, waste recycling projects seem especially badly served: there are no start-up grants of the kind available from the Department of Energy for local insulation projects.

Environmental project grants are also available from local authorities, trusts and under various campaign and award schemes such as the Shell Better Britain Campaign. Manchester City Council is the first local authority in Britain to introduce a Community Initiatives Fund, to which community groups and schools within the city can apply for grants of up to £25,000 (maximum for schools: £2,000) for environmental improvements to land and buildings.

In spite of all these sources, funding is often limited and uncertain for environmental projects in the voluntary sector. Some grants are only available if matched by cash from other sources (not materials, volunteers or other help in kind), so a great deal of effort goes into fund raising. To secure some types of funding, projects must continually demonstrate innovations – whereas the need locally may be for replication and consolidation. Organisations using MSC and Urban Programme monies have to reapply frequently and there are administrative difficulties over pooling finance. Getting money from European sources is time-consuming and often beyond the scope of small organisations, though some (like Landlife, with its training course in landscape design) have used the European Social Fund in imaginative ways.

Projects which aim to serve many objectives – environmental, social and economic – may find it difficult to raise funds in a system which categorises projects sharply. In theory, more funding sources become available, but much time can be spent seeking small sums from many places. Funding sources are needed which recognise and stimulate multi-objective schemes. Changes in the Urban Programme may help here: allocations will emphasise economic and environmental projects. But ratecapping, the decline in real value of the Urban Programme, and its restriction to 57 eligible authorities may further limit the UP sums going to voluntary sector schemes; they will need to stress economic objectives. In 1986/87, only 18 per cent of UP-funded voluntary projects were 'economic', 5 per cent were 'environmental'.[43]

Project staff interviewed noted that many funding sources provide capital for works and materials, but there are too few opportunities for revenue funding: for example, to pay for staff time to manage volunteers or to maintain a landscape that volunteers have created.

In a climate of greater competition for often dwindling funds, some projects are beginning to generate part of their needed income. Both the Urban Programme and the Community Programme have restrictive conditions on revenue generation which discourage enterprise. And it can be difficult to get feasibility and start-up support for new ventures. The case studies show that start-up supports (grants and low-interest, long-term loans) are particularly helpful for unconventional environmental businesses and to enable temporary projects to make the transition to providing more permanent jobs.[44] Yet it is not easy to get loans or advice specific to the needs of the new 'green' enterprises. Recognising this, the National Federation of City Farms is launching a revolving loan fund to support the development of community businesses on farms.

There are other problems when environmental initiatives aim to become more financially self-supporting – for some of the services they offer can never be income-earning. Trying to make them so can destroy the balance of objectives which ensures that community benefits are not sacrificed for short-term commercial success. Yet projects are vulnerable to shifts in the priorities for public spending. One way forward is for initiatives to charge for the environmental and social services they deliver – being paid in regular fees rather than grants – and for local authorities to contract with community organisations (as they are encouraged to do with the private sector) to provide more of these services. This already happens with the placement of mentally handicapped patients at some city farms. But there is scope for environmental initiatives to exploit more of their assets in this way.

STAFFING

Most of the projects described in this book were begun, and some are still sustained, by a small number of committed community entrepreneurs who provide the driving force and the vision. But the strengths needed to start up a community-based initiative are not the same as the administrative and business skills required to develop it – so project managers may need to change as a scheme grows. Even so, those interviewed acknowledged the advantages of continuing to involve initiators in some way.

Constantly changing personnel breaks a project's continuity – and this is a special problem for environmental schemes which rely mainly upon volunteers and upon temporary staff on special employment programmes. Where organisations take on temporary employees in MSC schemes, project management resources need to have continuity and be sufficient to provide adequate time and guidance for volunteers as well as paid staff.

TECHNICAL AID

All but the simplest environmental work will require some technical assistance and while information can be gleaned from an increasing number of handbooks, these are no substitute for specific advice. Some types of environmental scheme do have national co-ordinating bodies to provide technical advice and help with training and development. Neighbourhood Energy Action (NEA) and Energy Action Scotland do this for local energy projects, drawing on the expertise within the network. The National Federation of City Farms likewise co-ordinates city farms and community gardens, and Groundwork Trusts are members of the nationally-focussed Groundwork Foundation which helps the network in various ways. A new initiative – Waste Watch – has been set up to support community waste recycling schemes.

Better still, for local groups, is access to detailed, localised advice – not just on technical matters but on managerial and financial issues and on ways of involving a community. A number of the case studies point to the pivotal role that local technical aid centres (and other similar 'enabling' organisations) can play in the start-up of environmental schemes (see the Provost Estate, page 93 and Tower Hamlets Environment Trust, page 96). Not only do these offer a wide range of professional services (or access to them) but they can assist with their knowledge of local agencies and the political climate, and their negotiating skills. Manchester's Community Technical Aid Centre, in operation since 1979, helps local groups to get established (see *How to Start a Community Project*),[45] gives free advice on planning and landscape issues and provides architects for building work. CTAC can carry out feasibility studies and help groups to estimate costs and apply for funding.

Although there are now more than 70 technical aid centres in the UK, their distribution is patchy and incomplete. To be effective as community advocates and environmental counsellors, technical aid teams must be highly local. It has been difficult to find the funding for centres to start up. A National Community Aid Fund was launched in November 1986 to do this, but other funding sources are also needed which should include the Urban Programme, Urban Development Corporations and Task Forces.

There are, of course, dangers in all of this. Jeff Bishop notes how easy it is for professional groups, working to an assumed (but undefined) system of values, to influence a local group in subtle ways, destroying its spontaneity and responsiveness, and imposing

an 'acceptable' mode of environmental and community development which may not truly reflect local needs and wishes.[46]
Some of the case studies show that it is possible for enabling groups
to tread warily here, but this needs sensitivity, skill – and time (see
for example, the Provost Estate, page 93).

TRAINING

As groups and projects grow, they need in-house training, to
improve the quality of what they do, gain confidence and job satisfaction. Most of those interviewed complained of too few resources
here. Training is a sociable activity and gives identity to a project
and its staff. Volunteers as well as paid staff benefit from learning
not only specific skills but about the background and context for
their work – for example about the greening activities in other cities,
or progress in waste recycling. A number of the case studies point to
the value of trips organised to other projects for improving motivation and learning about good practice.

An increasing number of external training programmes are available to those running environmental projects. *Technical* training in
environmental work – hedging, walling, woodland and pond management – is well covered in courses and manuals produced by
agencies such as the British Trust for Conservation Volunteers, the
Tree Council, and the Woodland Trust. And co-ordinating bodies
like the National Federation of City Farms, NEA and the Groundwork Foundation, run special courses for their own members. Leadership and social skills training for those organising volunteers is
also well developed – by the Volunteer Centre, BTCV, the Countryside Commission and others.

But much of this training is oriented towards the countryside:
there is a need to incorporate material and examples drawn from
urban areas where the nature of the work – and workers – can be
very different. There is much to be learnt, especially on personnel
management, from training courses run for the voluntary social
services by the Volunteer Centre, volunteer bureaux and others, in
connection, for example, with the Opportunities for Volunteering
Programme. Environmental organisations need to seek out what is
relevant for their work.

Staff of many projects identify a lack of management and business
training focussed on the special problems of environmental schemes.
There are general courses (run, for example, by the National
Council for Voluntary Organisations), but there is a need for more
training on marketing, public relations, and the preparation of
business plans to attract funding and investment. More use could be
made of local educational institutions in developing appropriate
courses. Peter Kuenstler thinks that entirely new kinds of training,

blending business management with community relations, will have to be devised for 'community entrepreneurs'.[47]

Surprisingly, none of the projects studied had made use of the secondment of specialists – accountants and others – through agencies such as REACH (the Retired Executives Action Clearing House) and Action Resource Centre, both brokers for arranging secondments. But demand presently exceeds supply, and environmental groups cannot afford to buy in expensive business advice services.

EVALUATION OF PERFORMANCE

Some groups working on environmental schemes (the Groundwork Trusts for example) are beginning to define their objectives in more detail and devise performance standards as an aid to management, relating them not only to the quantity of environmental action (trees planted, wastes collected, homes insulated) but to the quality of the action (durability, community involvement, for example) and to the even less tangible notions of the quality of the experience offered to paid and voluntary workers. Effective evaluation of performance helps organisations to monitor their own progress, to report success and secure further funds. But evaluation requires a rigorous approach to identifying and assembling relevant information. None of the projects studied had developed this aspect of their work, though some were experimenting with social audits and ways of demonstrating value-for-money that go beyond financial cost-effectiveness to reflect wider social and environmental benefits.[48]

MANAGEMENT STRUCTURE

There seems to be a common pattern of development for many environmental organisations that engage in practical action. Volunteers play a critical role in stimulating and shaping the action. Paid staff are later taken on to implement and develop schemes and a period of conflicting objectives may result, where the aims of the original volunteers, new staff and users are all struggling to be represented. A management structure has to be found to accommodate these different interest groups. A limited liability charitable company (with its tax, rate and fund raising advantages) was the favoured structure, if necessary with a separate but related trading company. But groups acknowledged a need for advice on how to get the best from this structure, and especially on how to organise management committees effectively.

Those starting the new 'green' businesses favoured collective working – either in informal partnerships or as worker co-operatives (on which substantial local advice exists).

COMMUNITY INVOLVEMENT

Ideally this means responding to what a community wants to do, but few environmental initiatives claim to do this. Some (notably Ashram Acres and Windmill Hill City Farm) come close. With its elected management committee and full user participation in the way its activities are run, Windmill Hill has substantial community control. For Tower Hamlets Environment Trust, community development is a major objective of its work; the Trust maintains a continual dialogue with the local community (and its various components) through public meetings and consultations at every stage of a project. Special efforts are made to reach minority groups (page 100).

For most of the projects studied, community involvement means more than simply giving information. There may be informal contact with many local groups, talks in schools and special events. For greening schemes, active participation is acknowledged to be the key to reducing vandalism and enlisting support for continuing management. Well-organised celebrations – occasions for simply having fun – are valuable ways of building and sustaining local commitment to a project. But these take time, have to be planned and budgetted for – all agreed that effective community involvement never 'just happens'. The Free Form Arts Trust thinks as much patience, imagination and testing of alternatives are needed here as in technical matters. Project staff have to be flexible enough in their forward programmes to accommodate this, and confident in their attitudes towards community involvement in environmental action: that the process can be as important as the product.

Art is a growing theme for participation in environmental work. Cardiff City Farm is one of a number of local initiatives now hosting an 'artist in residence' (in this case a potter) to explore with people the links between art and environment.

RELATIONS WITH OTHER AGENCIES

The more successful schemes have many local links to draw upon for information, advice, funds, materials, markets and personnel. Most of the case studies show the value of building close links with local authorities whose departments can supply funds (directly and by leverage), tools and vehicles. They can often negotiate (or provide) land and premises, storage space, legal advice and insurance cover. And some allow local groups to use council facilities – for printing and publicity, or rooms for meeting.

In turn, environmental projects in the voluntary sector can be influential in changing local authority policies and practice. (See, for example, Tower Hamlets Environment Trust, page 97.) In some authorities the partnership has been especially effective: in Newcastle, for example, the local energy project 'Keeping Newcastle

Warm' is supported financially by the council and has become one part of a comprehensive policy on energy efficiency in the city. Similarly, treated as partners, community recycling schemes can help local authorities to develop their policies on waste management (see CSAWS, page 55).

But there are problems for voluntary sector schemes in knowing which department to contact: environmental projects can be of interest to planning, housing, social services, leisure and recreation, environmental health, education and economic development. And some projects need to relate to more than one department: Moulson notes that the job creation and enterprise potential of recycling schemes will not be explored if these are the concern only of public works, or environmental health departments.[49] As part of its programme to develop partnerships between local authorities and energy projects, NEA is urging councils to designate contact officers or set up inter-departmental working groups to provide a clear channel of communication on energy issues.[50] Liaison officers for other activities are needed.[51]

Even those authorities who accept that the voluntary sector has a part to play in local economic development will need persuading that environmental projects, too, can be a focus for regeneration, yet the recommendations in NCVO's report *Joint Action – The Way Forward* are just as relevant for these projects.[52] Ideally, they need a number of services from a 'one stop' development agency that could provide start-up support (feasibility studies, loans and grants, help with premises, legal and business advice) and on-going support (on training, injections of working capital, for example) – but all with a recognition of the environmental dimension. More local authorities, working with other public agencies locally, could play this role, but their involvement with less conventional enterprises is still largely experimental.[53]

Some projects have made good links with the private sector, receiving help in a variety of ways: donations from the company and its employees (perhaps through payroll giving); underwriting of loans; staff secondments; sponsorship of events, buildings, schemes and publications; and gifts of goods and equipment. Building materials, trees and uniforms have all been given to local groups featured in the case studies, and many thought there was much more scope for company giving – and some for company buying.[54]

To make and enhance local links, projects need to cultivate good relations with the media and produce lively publicity, circulated to firms and local authorities with invitations to visit. For their part, these local agencies need to respond. The case studies confirm that these visits increase morale, and can lead to mutually beneficial action, but groups are frustrated by the lack of response to their invitations.

More local fora are needed where public, private and voluntary organisations can meet to inform each other, exchange views, and plan collaboration, for example, on the supply of goods and services. Voluntary Initiatives on Vacant Land (VIVA) and the North East Environment Network are two examples of coalitions of local groups, others are the West Midlands Environment Network (formery 'Think Green') and the Merseyside Environment Trust. Some initiatives (notably city farms) have already made useful contacts with their counterparts in Europe; many advantages could flow from greater international exchange of experience and personnel.

SUMMING UP

The evidence is that community-based environmental action can provide good opportunities for voluntary and paid work, with scope for people to develop their personalities, their confidence and their skills. And the jobs that flow from these initiatives often reach the more disadvantaged in the labour market. There are signs of new 'green enterprises' emerging, and although their scale is presently small, it is likely that these could grow if some of the obstacles to their development were removed and the movement was encouraged.

All these pioneering initiatives – like many others in the voluntary sector – display attitudes and ways of working which have a permanent part to play in urban regeneration. They are not just plugging gaps in the array of public and private sector services (though they often do this too).

There are certainly weaknesses. But the strengths lie in their sensitivity to local needs, their willingness and flexibility to respond in many different ways, their capacity to be experimental and to harness people's creativity and enthusiasm for local action. These are not temporary values.

More and more local authorities are realising the advantages of working closely with community organisations – not least to make use of their expertise and their ability to reach people directly. Businesses too, increasingly concerned to project a corporate image of environmental and social responsibility, have much to learn from the voluntary sector; some are contributing in a variety of ways.

However, if the community contribution to urban regeneration is to grow and become more effective, then extra support is needed. Among the priorities emerging from this study must be:

- fostering further co-operation between voluntary groups and the public and business sectors – enabling central government agencies such as Urban Development Corporations, Task Forces and City Action Teams, the enterprise agencies (and other members of Business in the Community), and local authorities to work closely with local groups, using environmental action, where appropriate, as a stimulus for regeneration;

- improving the access that local groups have to technical and business advice and training – through their own networks, other local support agencies, and secondments;

- greater continuity of public funding and easier access to finance for experimental 'green' enterprises to start up and employ local people;

- further improvements in the organisation of government employment programmes to foster training, volunteer management and enterprise development;

- closer working between neighbouring voluntary sector initiatives, with the pooling of resources and sharing of expertise to increase effectiveness and ensure that the 'third force' becomes a recognisable element of urban regeneration;

- more opportunities for project staff and volunteers to exchange experience and learn from each other – both in the UK and elsewhere.

The new vision is that citizens themselves have the skills and imagination to green the city. But they need practical help, not just good will.

Provost Estate

13 Green fingers on the Provost Estate, Hackney.

On this inter-war estate of 250 flats in Hackney, North London, the Tenants' Association worked with a technical aid centre – the Free Form Arts Trust – to improve greenspace between the housing blocks, build a mural and introduce window boxes.

Until 1986, the estate, which is now owned by Hackney Borough Council, was the property of the Greater London Council which was responsible for environmental work. In 1982, the GLC announced a Community Areas Policy – under which its tenants could bid for funds to carry out estate improvements. There was already a GLC brief for environmental work at Provost, but this did not incorporate what the tenants felt was needed. The once-grassed areas around the housing blocks had become seas of mud as people had followed the shortest route between their homes: paved pathways, seats and lighting were all priorities. And there was little variety of aspect and no relief from drab brick walls; the tenants especially wanted some environmental improvements around the ground floor 'community flat' which they use as the base for a variety of social events.

Some of the tenants knew of Free Form's work in neighbouring boroughs and approached the group for advice. At a public meeting, attended by representatives of the Tenants' Association, the GLC, Hackney Borough Council's Housing Department and Free Form, it was decided that Free Form, acting as the GLC's agent, would design and cost a scheme for the tenants to comment upon and that the GLC would produce a leaflet on the proposals for distribution to all the tenants for their comments.

It took many meetings and months to work out a compromise with dominating, sometimes opposing, and constantly changing members of the Tenants' Association. Free Form's Hazel Goldman needed all the patience and ingenuity she had developed on other projects to enable tenants to reach agreement. New designs were continually produced and discussed in response to their ideas. 'This was', she remembers, 'a time-consuming but necessary stage. It was essential for Free Form to inform as many residents as possible about the plans, and to act as mediator – and sometimes scapegoat – to get a well-supported decision that had some chance of working in practice.'

To show results quickly, and so persuade all the tenants to feel involved, Free Form proposed that each home might have a window box to brighten up the access balconies. These were free and adopted by a majority of tenants in 1984. A choice of plants, requiring different amounts of care, was offered and those tenants who wished went to the nursery to select plants. Now, two years on, most of the window boxes are still well-tended, and they make an immediate impact upon the environment of the estate. There are now many more birds around, and in some window boxes, to the delight of their owners, birds have nested. 'That made a lot of people happy' says Mary Walker, secretary of the Tenants' Association.

Other improvements so far (installed by contractors working to the community designs eventually agreed) include new paved walkways, some varied shrub planting, wooden seats and new lights. The designs are unusual and effective. New railings to protect vegetation, ground floor windows and climbing plants have been specially designed and constructed by an ironsmith: they are functional works of art. Vandalism and unwitting damage to plants have been prevented. The seats are well used, especially by the older residents who now talk more and feel less isolated. The scale is intimate: 'something you can relate to' they say.

On a wall facing the community flat, tenants joined with Free Form designers to build an unusual mural which depicts local peoples' ideas about the river Thames and the docks. Many local children were involved in the mural-making, developing, with Free Form, new ways of building up relief, making moulds and casts of their toys which were added to the wall. At first, there was opposition to all of this, residents did not want a painted mural which they felt would wear badly and was expensive. But the idea which eventually emerged is robust, attractive, and now welcomed by the majority. Completion of the mural was celebrated in 1984 with a Hallowe'en party.

Overall grant aid for the scheme was £56,000. 'It helped,' says Hazel Goldman, 'to keep people well informed about how the money was being spent – itemised costs for each stage were posted near the community flat'.

These green environments on the estate, achieved by Free Form in detailed negotiations with tenants, contrast starkly with adjacent GLC landscaping, completed later. Here, there was only token consultation, ideas contributed by residents were not incorporated. The paving is uniform and sterile, the planting has been quite severely damaged. Elsewhere on the estate, an old people's garden, like a prisoners' compound with backless seats turned away from the street, lies desolate and unused save for glue-sniffers and junkies.

Free Form's work on the Provost Estate is typical of their approach to involving people in the improvement of their neighbourhoods – the *process* of environmental change is seen to be as important as the *product*. The philosophy is that people know best what is needed and they can be helped to express and celebrate their own intuitive creativity.

Tower Hamlets Environment Trust

14 Terry Lyle, the Education Officer of Tower Hamlets Environment Trust and children from Chisenhale school in the East End.

15 Armagh Road, Tower Hamlets – a Community Land Use project.

This community-based organisation has improved many acres of wasteland, organised popular cultural events, become an effective voice for local people on environmental and development issues and has substantial influence over local authority policies. All of this has happened in a London borough with some of the worst social problems of the capital. Dot Deeming, a trustee, describes it as 'a terrible environment to live in'.

Tower Hamlets Environment Trust (THET) was established in 1979 by planning consultants Benson and Wilcox Associates as a pilot project in local environmental improvement, funded first by the GLC and then the Urban Programme, through the London Borough of Tower Hamlets. The Trust was incorporated with four trustees and began projects in Aldgate, but it had no permanent staff until 1981, when Jon Aldenton was appointed as development officer. The Trust then began to work with tenants and other local groups on the environmental improvement of housing estates and wasteland.

During its first five years the Trust improved over 50 sites in the borough, set up environmental education programmes in local schools, insulated many homes and steadily increased its role as an access point for the community on environmental issues.

Early on, the Trust developed an approach of multiple objectives. Though priorities have changed, and the definition of environment has widened in response to public concerns and the arrival of staff with a range of skills, this linking of objectives remains. The Trust is concerned with environmental improvement, community involvement, increasing employment and local economic activity. It operates directly, through its own staff, through the associated (though increasingly independent) agency Community Land Use (CLU) and in partnership with others.

What it does

Continuing its early work, the Trust is co-ordinating an improvement scheme in Aldgate, the entrance to the borough, which has important historic and commercial assets, but is marred by litter, poor maintenance and limited pedestrian access. THET provided the launch and publicity, began a litter bin sponsorship scheme, has organised site action and community consultations and brought public, private and community interests together in a Steering Group. The project is part-funded from the Tower Hamlets Inner Area Programme; extra funds are raised through private sector sponsorship and advertising.

But most of the Trust's practical environmental work has involved helping local groups to transform vacant land into play areas, amenity greenspace, nature gardens (especially on school grounds), roof gardens and allotments. One example is the Attlee Adventure Playground which was upgraded with facilities for disabled children – a specialism which CLU have developed on a number of sites. Beginning in 1984, another site, Armagh Road was transformed in stages into a ribbon of open space incorporating a park, tree nursery, play area and nature garden. And allotments now flourish in the once-derelict Cable Street Community Garden.

The Trust has worked hard in other ways to support community gardening. It has helped the borough council to establish its Community Gardening Programme (with an annual budget of £300,000) under which more than 25 community greening projects have been implemented. Since 1983, THET's Hanbury Street base has housed the small Brady Garden and Nursery which grows trees and flowers in containers for local groups to plant on their sites. Recycled garden materials are also collected here and a nursery of young trees is maintained at Mudchute Farm for groups to use. The Trust and the borough's community gardener are co-operating on a long-term project – Trees for Tower Hamlets – to encourage the planting, aftercare and appreciation of trees and shrubs. Householders, shop keepers, businesses, tenants' and residents' associations, schools and churches are all offered free trees and climbers.

Linked to the wasteland projects is THET's concern for environmental education. Terry Lyle, the Trust's lively education officer, works with children in more than 60 schools and with many community groups, not only to create simple landscapes but to respond to their enthusiasm for learning about natural history and conservation. Terry spends much time talking with groups before they start work on a site. He may draw up schemes with them, and help them to organise the action and the maintenance (lending tools, providing plants and motivating volunteers). Acknowledging that continuing management can be a problem, he visits schemes at least twice each year and keeps groups in touch with each other to share problems.

Community Land Use – the Trust's associated technical aid agency – has helped many local groups to renovate buildings and put up new community facilities. Projects have included hard and soft landscaping on housing estates, a purpose-built play centre, and the refurbishment of several youth clubs.

Promoting East End culture is seen as another important role for the Trust. It has researched and produced leaflets on local walks, the 'East End Music Halls' and its 'Parks and Farms' and has placed commemorative plaques celebrating famous political figures and events in the borough. More are planned. In 1985, working with the council, THET organised an exhibition and related events about the Huguenots in the East End which ran for five weeks and attracted 6,000 people. The Trust raised £12,000 from various sources, partly refurbished a disused building in Spitalfields and prepared teaching materials for schools. A more ambitious festival: 'Jewish East End Celebration' with many events and exhibitions ran successfully over the summer of 1987.

As well as these practical projects, THET aims to influence planning and development in the borough on behalf of its residents: by consultation with the community (informally, and through public meetings), by commenting on policy documents and development applications and by representing community groups at inquiries. In this work, THET interprets 'environment' widely to include retail and office development, housing and recreation.

Since 1985, work on planning and development issues has increased with the preparation of a community plan for a major development site in Whitechapel. The Trust co-ordinated briefs and submissions, organised public consultations, negotiated throughout with the council and local groups, and set up the Whitechapel Development Trust in 1986 as an independent company to implement the plan. Although this was not, in the end, approved, the Whitechapel Development Trust will now implement smaller housing and industrial schemes adjacent to the main development site. It is through this project that the Trust has extended its influence over local policies, forcing the council to consider alternatives, to organise full public consultations and to revise its own briefs.

Wherever possible, the Trust aims to link economic development with environmental improvement – both indirectly in its work on community plans (ensuring, for example, no loss of industrial floorspace, promoting small workshops) and directly. In 1985 CLU designed a robust litter bin which is now manufactured by an East End firm and, following a commendation from the Design Council, is being marketed nationwide.

How the Trust works

THET is a charitable company with a 10–person management committee representing the council, trades union, ethnic minority, youth and other community interests. The Trust's corporate identity is set by its staff, and especially by its development officer, Jon Aldenton, a psychology graduate with a background in community work and trade union affairs. He sets the democratic style of response to local people and lobbies skilfully on their behalf through many local networks, using his contacts and knowledge of council affairs. An increasingly professional team (four full-time, three part-time) is managed to make the most of their specialist skills: in planning, local history and environmental education.

Funding for the Trust now comes mainly from the London Borough of Tower Hamlets: in 1986 £38,600 under the Inner Area Programme and £10,000 mainstream. £23,000 came (via CLU) from fees. The London Boroughs Grant Scheme provided £50,000 for the CLU technical aid service and other consultants and £15,000 came from the ILEA for THET's education work. Smaller sums have been raised from the private sector for particular projects. Because of the uncertainty over future funding when the Inner Area Programme finishes in 1988, the Trust is looking for ways of generating revenue from development projects.

The Trust's work has spawned two co-operatives: Community Land Use and Warmth.

Community Land Use (CLU)

From 1982–3, 26 workers were funded under the Community Enterprise Programme (CEP) to provide skills and resources to community groups to carry out practical environmental projects and develop environmental understanding, especially in schools. From April 1983, the GLC supported a four-person professional team to act as a technical aid service for local groups and by 1985, CLU was handling contracts valued at £500,000 and expected to become self-financing. A six-person co-operative of architects and landscape architects was formed in 1985.

Now managed independently, earning £60,000 in fee income from projects, CLU maintains a continuing relationship with THET. The

Trust employs (from its London Boroughs Grants fund) some of the CLU staff to work on grant-aided projects, and receives from CLU a fee to cover the costs of THET work on schemes which are subsequently managed by CLU (£23,000 in 1986). This work usually concerns fund raising and THET is able to help with its wider perspective, its knowledge of local interests and experience of previous schemes.

Warmth
Beginning in 1982 as an MSC scheme, Warmth grew to a 12–person co-operative insulating homes in three London boroughs and on GLC housing estates. The demise of the GLC and a lack of promotion to win further contracts has resulted in Warmth now having only one part-time employee.

Community involvement
Both THET and CLU are committed to a philosophy of responding to local concerns on a wide range of environmental issues, and maintaining a continual process of involvement with local groups – from a project idea, through consultation on alternative designs and implementation, to management. In the Trust's experience, this approach fosters local commitment to action, helps in the maintenance of sites and contributes to the wider ideals of community development.

The Trust aims to maintain a sensitivity to issues of concern as they arise. 'We try', says Jon Aldenton, 'to express people's grumbles as needs, and respond early on rather than at the firefighting stage'. Both THET and CLU, in their detailed operations, try to articulate and meet the special needs of different groups: for example, by printing information in Bengali, organising meetings for women or by designing facilities for disabled people. Trustee Dot Deeming feels that the THET board now represents well the different community interests at stake in the borough and that the Trust as a whole, particularly through its staff, is excellent at reflecting local concern about the environment. It provides, she says, a valuable access point for groups to communicate their views. 'The main thing about the Trust is it gets things done. It listens to what people say – and the council listens to the Trust.'

In future, THET wants to increase its involvement in development proposals, emphasising housing needs and local regeneration. Wasteland work will continue, but probably more slowly as land values continue to rise, and perhaps with the Trust encouraging local management groups to form. More traffic problems – road building, pollution and poor public transport – are likely to be tackled.

Summing up
The Trust has been successful in what it does and how it works. It

has a track record of action on the ground showing what can be achieved by the community. People benefit directly from the projects which would not otherwise have taken place: many acres of greenspace created, new and refurbished community buildings, successful exhibitions and festivals. In all these ways the Trust demonstrates a concern for *enjoying* the environment as well as improving it, fostering local pride in the East End and its cultures. The Whitechapel Community Plan has increased the Trust's confidence that it has the professional capacity to act on major issues.

THET has a reputation for successful mediation with councillors and council departments, for speeding up projects and getting money for them. It operates in the interstices of local groups, bringing different interests together: not many local organisations have the flexibility to act this way.

THET has had a major influence on local authority practice. By being experimental and persistent, the Trust has been able to initiate and sustain borough interest in environmental issues and influence wider planning and development policies.

References

1 INTRODUCTION

1 Knevitt, Charles. *Community Enterprise, The Times*/Calouste Gulbenkian Foundation, 1986.

National Council for Voluntary Organisations (NCVO). *Joint Action – The Way Forward: Community Involvement in Local Economic Development*, Bedford Square Press/NCVO, 1984.

Town and Country Planning Association. *Whose Responsibility? Reclaiming the Inner Cities*, TCPA, 1986.

Vincent, K. 'Community Based Responses to Unemployment' in *Unemployment Strategies*, The Alternative Employment Group in Scotland, 1984.

2 Kuenstler, Peter. *Community Action to Combat Unemployment: The Contribution of Local Employment Initiatives*, Commission of the European Communities, 1983.

McArthur, Andrew. *The Community Business Movement in Scotland: Contributions, Public Sector Responses and Possibilities*, Centre for Urban and Regional Research, University of Glasgow Discussion Paper 17, 1984.

Various authors. *Communities in Business*, Centre for Employment Initiatives for Community Initiatives Research Trust, 1986.

NCVO. *Joint Action*, op.cit., 1984.

Robertson, James. 'The Economics of Local Recovery', Paper to the Other Economic Summit (TOES), 1986.

3 Davidson, Joan and MacEwen, Ann. *The Livable City*, Royal Institute of British Architects, 1983.

4 Lowe, Phillip and Goyder, Jane. *Environmental Groups in Politics*, Allen and Unwin, 1983.

5 Davies, Robert. 'Conservation Through the Back Door' in *Town and Country Planning*, September 1983.

6 O'Riordan, Tim. 'What Does Sustainability Really Mean?', Paper for CEED Conference on Sustainable Development in an Industrial Economy, 1985.

7 Morris, David. *The New City States*, Institute for Local Self Reliance, Washington, 1982.

Cordova-Novion, C. and Sachs, Céline. *Urban Self-Reliance Directory*, International Foundation for Development Alternatives, 1987.

Redclift, Michael and Porritt, Jonathan. 'Why Bankrupt the Earth?', Paper to The Other Economic Summit (TOES), 1986.

8 Labour Party. *Jobs and Environment* – Second Interim Report, Labour Party, 1986.

9 Dartington Institute and British Trust for Conservation Volunteers. 'Work and the Environment', unpublished report for the Department of the Environment, 1986.

10 Rankin, Mark. 'Working in the margin – unemployment, volunteering and marginal work', Discussion Paper, The Volunteer Centre, 1985.

2   LOCAL ENVIRONMENTAL ACTION

11 Bradley, Christine. *Community Involvement in Greening Projects*, Groundwork Foundation, 1986.
See also:
Department of Environment. *Greening City Sites: Good Practice in Urban Regeneration*, HMSO, 1987.
Nicholas-Lord, David. *The Greening of the Cities*, Routledge and Kegan Paul, 1987.

12 Dawe, Gerald. 'Urban Habitat Creation: Some Points in Practice', *Ecos* 5(4), 1984.

13 Elkington, John. *Groundwork – The Environmental Entrepreneurs*, Groundwork Foundation, 1986.

14 Neighbourhood Energy Action. *Coming in from the Cold*, NEA, 1985.

15 Gordon, Jo. *Waste Recycling in the Community*, NCVO, 1987.
See also *Resource*, the Quarterly Review of Reclamation, Re-use and Recycling, Avon Friends of the Earth, Bristol.

16 Moulson, Richard and Newson, John. 'Jobs from Waste: the Potential in Birmingham', unpublished report of Friends of the Earth Birmingham to Birmingham City Council, 1986.

3   STARTING UP, KEEPING GOING

17 Nabarro, Rupert; Davies, Robert; Cobbold, Chris; and Galley, Nora. *Local Enterprise and the Unemployed*, Calouste Gulbenkian Foundation, 1986.

18 Kuenstler, Peter. 'Conclusions' in *Communities in Business*, Centre for Employment Initiatives, 1986.

19 Watling, Trevor. *Report of the First London Community Business Conference*, London Voluntary Service Council, 1986.
See also:
National Federation of City Farms. 'Community Businesses for City Farms – a Way Forward', unpublished report, NFCF, 1987.

20 McArthur, Andrew. op.cit., 1984.

21 Department of the Environment. *Creating Development Trusts: Good Practice in Urban Regeneration*, HMSO, 1988.

4   MAKING THE MOST OF VOLUNTEERING

22 Humble, Stephen. *Voluntary Action in the 1980s*, The Volunteer Centre, 1982.

23 Gerard, David. 'What Makes a Volunteer?', *New Society*, 8 November 1985.

Field, Julia and Hedges, Barry. *A National Survey of Volunteering*, report of Social and Community Planning Research, 1984.

24 Pettigrew, Wendy. *Involving Volunteers in the Environment*, The Volunteer Centre, 1985.

25 Stubbings, Peter. 'Central Government Policies towards Volunteers: Some Guiding Principles', Volunteer Centre Policy Discussion Document, 1983.

26 Association of Community Technical Aid Centres. *Releasing Community Initiative*, Information Pack, published by ACTAC, 1986.

27 The Volunteer Centre. *Guidelines for Relationships between Volunteers and Paid Non-professional Workers* ('Drain Guidelines'), 1977.

28 See, for example, McCullough, Jamie. *Meanwhile Gardens*, Calouste Gulbenkian Foundation, 1978.

29 Bradley, Christine. op. cit., 1986.

30 Ford, Kevin. *A Matter of Choice: Unemployment, Volunteering and Volunteer Bureaux*, published by Project VBx, 1985.

31 Stubbings, Peter. *Work and Unemployment in the Countries of the EEC*, European Commission, 1985.

32 Bishop, Jeff, and Hoggett, Paul. *Organizing around Enthusiasms*, Comedia Publishing Group, 1986.

33 Hatch, Stephen and Gay, Pat. *Making the Best of Being Out of Work*, Research Report on the Voluntary Projects Programme, Manpower Services Commission, 1984.

34 Rankin, M. op. cit., 1985.

5   MORE JOBS, NEW ENTERPRISE

35 McArthur, Andrew. op. cit., 1984.

36 Normington, David; Brodie, Hugh; and Munro, Jim. *Value for Money in the Community Programme*, Manpower Services Commission, 1986.

37 National Task Group on the Community Programme. *A Better Community Programme*, NCVO, 1987.

38 McArthur, Andrew. op. cit., 1984.

39 Nabarro, Rupert; Davies, Robert; Cobbold, Chris; and Galley, Nora. *Local Enterprise and the Unemployed*, op. cit., 1986.

40 Moulson, Richard and Newson, John. 'Jobs from Waste: the Potential in Birmingham', op. cit., 1986.

41 'Off the Dole' in *Energy Action* 17, December 1985.

6 MAKING IT HAPPEN

42 Macclesfield Groundwork Trust. *Raising Money for Environmental Improvement*, Shell Better Britain Campaign, 1986.

43 Davies, A. 'A Voice in the City', *New Society*, 27 March 1987.

44 See also Nabarro, Rupert; Davies, Robert; Cobbold, Chris; and Galley, Nora. *Local Enterprise and the Unemployed*, op. cit., 1986.

45 Community Technical Aid Centre. *How to Start a Community Project*, CTAC Manchester, 1987.
See also:
Annual Report 1985/86, published by CTAC Manchester.
Manchester City Council, Partnership Ltd, Think Green. *Community Landscapes*, a pack of ideas and case studies available from Think Green, Birmingham, 1986.

46 Bishop, Jeff and Hoggett, Paul. op. cit., 1986.

47 Kuenstler, Peter. op. cit., 1986.

48 See, for example, Feek, Warren. *Working Effectively: A Guide to Evaluation Techniques*, Bedford Square Press/NCVO, 1988.

49 Moulson, Richard and Newson, John. op. cit., 1986.

50 Neighbourhood Energy Action. *Keeping Out the Cold*, NEA, 1987.

51 NCVO. 'Local Government – Use It, Don't Abuse It': Report of a seminar for environmental voluntary groups. 1987.

52 NCVO. *Joint Action*: op. cit., 1984.
See also:
Edwards, Ken. 'A Vigorous Minority' in *New Society*, 10 April 1987.

53 Allan, Malcolm. 'Local Authorities and Economic Development' in *Initiatives*, vol 4(1), February 1987.

54 Logan, David. 'Future Prospects' (for corporate social responsibility) in *Initiatives*, vol 4(5), October 1987.

Organisations and Programmes

This list includes organisations and programmes referred to in the text.

Action Resource Centre (ARC)
CAP House, 9–11 Long Lane
London EC1A 9HD
Tel: 01 726 8987
Independent charity which provides business advice and specialists on secondment from companies to voluntary organisations.

Association of Community Technical Aid Centres (ACTAC)
The Royal Institution
Colquitt Street
Liverpool L1 4DE
Tel: 051 708 7607
National co-ordinating body for community technical aid centres which offer free or low cost professional advice to local groups on architecture, planning, design, finance and other issues involved in the community improvement of land and buildings.

British Trust For Conservation Volunteers (BTCV)
36 St Mary's Street
Wallingford
Oxfordshire OX10 0EU
Tel: 0491 39766
Provides and organises volunteers for practical conservation projects through 12 regional offices; gives advice and information on recruiting volunteers and runs training courses. There are 370 BTCV local groups.

Community Service Volunteers (CSV)
237 Pentonville Road
London N1 9NJ
Tel: 01 278 6601
Places young people (18–30) in full-time volunteer posts for up to a year in the social services, conservation and the local media. Volunteers receive board, lodging, pocket money and expenses. CSV runs training courses and Community Programme schemes.

Community Programme (CP)
Temporary employment programme of the Manpower Services Commission (MSC) for long-term unemployed people to work for up to 52 weeks on projects which benefit the community.

Councils for Voluntary Service (CVS)
Co-ordinate, support and develop voluntary sector action locally, and act as centres of information and advice. Details from NCVO.

Enterprise Allowance
Offers long-term unemployed people (or those recently on the Community Programme) an allowance of £40 per week while they try to start a business. £1,000 capital is required.

Enterprise Projects
In the Community Programme, Enterprise Projects allow participants in some MSC pilot areas to try out a business idea while still on the CP. Allows commercial trading in the last three months, with extra funds for training and advice.

Groundwork Foundation
Bennetts Court
6 Bennetts Hill
Birmingham B2 5ST

Tel: 021 236 8565

National co-ordinating body for groundwork trusts – a network of independent local trusts working with industry, local authorities and voluntary organisations to improve the urban and urban edge environment.

Job Training Scheme (JTS)

For 18–25 year olds, unemployed for 6–12 months. Trainees receive appropriate benefit rate plus travelling expenses.

Manpower Services Commission (MSC)

Moorfoot
Sheffield S1 4PQ
Tel: 0742 753275

Government job creation agency providing temporary employment and training under a number of schemes, including the Community Programme and Voluntary Projects Programme.

National Council for Voluntary Organisations (NCVO)

26 Bedford Square
London WC1B 3HU
Tel: 01 636 4066

Represents and provides a variety of services for its membership of voluntary organisations in England, including legal advice, management training, liaison with government departments, and conferences.

National Federation of City Farms (NFCF)

The Old Vicarage
66 Fraser Street
Bedminster
Bristol BS3 4LY
Tel: 0272 660663

National co-ordinating body for city farms and community gardens; provides information, advice and training.

Neighbourhood Energy Action (NEA)

2/4 Bigg Market
Newcastle-upon-Tyne NE1 1UW

Tel: 091 261 5677

Co-ordinating body in England and Wales for local energy projects which offer insulation and advice for low-income families. Gives information, advice and training. Energy Action Scotland co-ordinates schemes in Scotland.

Opportunities for Volunteering

A scheme run by the Department of Health and Social Services for unemployed people to do voluntary work on projects in the field of health and personal social services.

Retired Executives Action Clearing House (REACH)

89 Southwark Street
London SE1 0HD
Tel: 01 928 0452

Acts as a link to bring retired executives from business and industry to work (usually for expenses only) for voluntary organisations.

Think Green

Premier House
43–48 New Street
Birmingham B2 4LJ
Tel: 021 643 8899

A three-year nationwide campaign for greener towns and cities, which promotes festivals and celebrations in particular cities and fosters the formation of local 'think green' networks.

UK 2000

2–3 Horse and Dolphin Yard
Macclesfield Street
London W1V 7LG
Tel: 01 631 5160

A partnership initiative between the business, government and voluntary sectors to create new jobs improving the environment. Projects are carried out by volunteers and by workers on the MSC Community Programme.

Voluntary Projects Programme (VPP)

An MSC voluntary work programme for unemployed people to

train in new skills. Participants are unpaid but can receive expenses.

Volunteer Bureaux (VBx)
Local agencies (run by paid staff and volunteers) which stimulate and support voluntary work, maintain contact with the organisations that use volunteers and try to place volunteers in posts appropriate to their interests and capabilities. Details from the Volunteer Centre.

Volunteer Centre
29 Lower King's Road
Berkhamsted
Herts HP4 2AB
Tel: 044 27 73311
National advisory centre on volunteering and community involvement. Co-ordinates the network of 250 volunteer bureaux. Runs the Crossover Project which encourages companies to collaborate on schemes of part-time paid release for older employees to do voluntary work.

Waste Watch
26 Bedford Square
London WC1B 3HU
Tel: 01 636 4066
National campaign to promote recycling and support community-based recycling schemes.

Case Studies

Ashram Acres
Ashram Community Service Project
23–25 Grantham Road
Sparkbrook
Birmingham B11 1LU
Tel: 021 773 7061

**Avon Friends of the Earth
(AVON FOE)**
Arno's Castle Estate
Junction Road
Brislington
Bristol BS4
Tel: 0272 715446

Blackwall Products Ltd
Unit 4
Riverside Industrial Estate
River Way
London SE10 0BE
Tel: 01 305 1431

Bristol Energy Centre
Philip Street
Bedminster
Bristol BS3 4DR
Tel: 0272 633895

Camden Garden Centre
66 Kentish Town Road
London NW1 8NY
Tel: 01 485 8468

Camden Recycling Ltd
Cockpit Yard
Northington Street
London WC1N 2NP
Tel: 01 242 0157

Cardiff City Farm
Sloper Road
Grangetown
Cardiff CF1 8AB
Tel: 0222 384360

**Community Support Anti-Waste
Scheme (CSAWS)**
Ty Ail-Law
1 Hope Terrace
Cardiff CF2 2AU
Tel: 0222 465365

Free Form Arts Trust
38 Dalston Lane
London E8 3AZ
Tel: 01 249 3394

Growth Unlimited
Voluntary Action Camden
25–31 Tavistock Place
London WC1
Tel: 01 388 2071

Hackney Brass Tacks
18 Ashwin Street
London E8 3DL
Tel: 01 249 9461

Hackney Grove Garden
Contact Free Form Arts Trust

Keeping Newcastle Warm
1 Charlotte Square
Newcastle-upon-Tyne NE1 4XF
Tel: 091 261 5555

Landlife
Old Police Station
Lark Lane
Liverpool L17 8UU
Tel: 051 728 7011

Landwise
8 Elliot Place
Glasgow G3 8EP
Tel: 041 248 3993

**Oldham and Rochdale Ground-
work Trust**
Bank House
8 Chapel Street
Shaw
Oldham OL2 8AJ
Tel: 0706 842212

Paperback Ltd
8–16 Coronet Street
London N1 6HD
Tel: 01 729 1382

Provost Estate
Contact Free Form Arts Trust

Sholver Rangers
Contact Oldham and Rochdale
Groundwork Trust

Tower Hamlets Environment Trust (THET)
Brady Centre
192–6 Hanbury Street
London E1 5HU
01 377 0481

Urban Centre for Appropriate Technology (UCAT)
Contact Bristol Energy Centre

Windmill Hill City Farm
Doveton Street
off Philip Street
Bedminster
Bristol BS3 4DU
Tel: 0272 633252